SAILING RIGS

An Illustrated Guide

Jenny Bennett
Drawings by Veres László

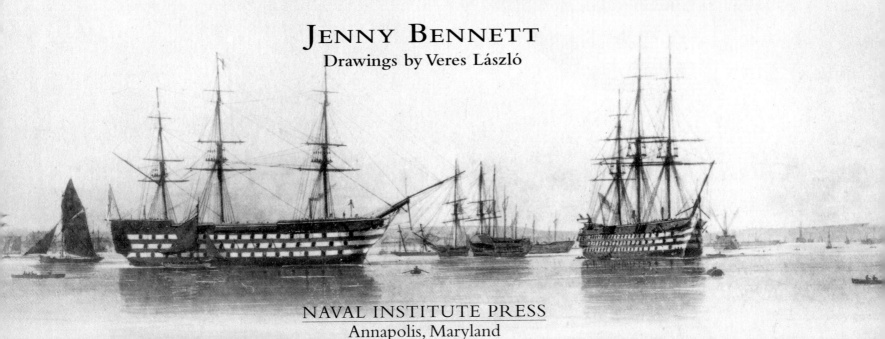

NAVAL INSTITUTE PRESS
Annapolis, Maryland

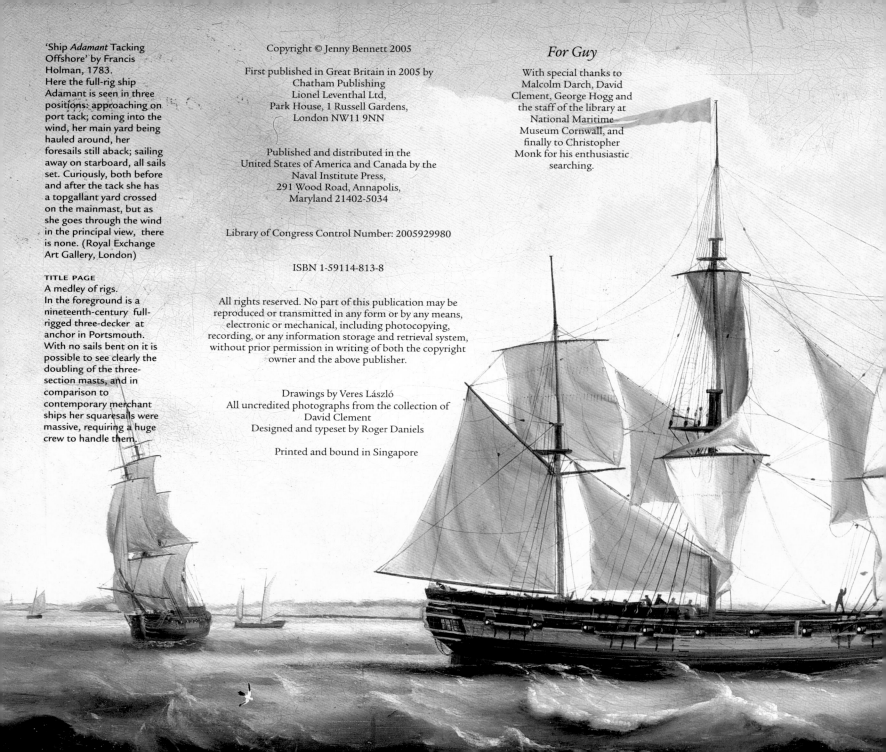

'Ship *Adamant* Tacking Offshore' by Francis Holman, 1783. Here the full-rig ship *Adamant* is seen in three positions: approaching on port tack; coming into the wind, her main yard being hauled around, her foresails still aback; sailing away on starboard, all sails set. Curiously, both before and after the tack she has a topgallant yard crossed on the mainmast, but as she goes through the wind in the principal view, there is none. (Royal Exchange Art Gallery, London)

TITLE PAGE
A medley of rigs.
In the foreground is a nineteenth-century full-rigged three-decker at anchor in Portsmouth. With no sails bent on it is possible to see clearly the doubling of the three-section masts, and in comparison to contemporary merchant ships her squaresails were massive, requiring a huge crew to handle them.

Copyright © Jenny Bennett 2005

First published in Great Britain in 2005 by
Chatham Publishing
Lionel Leventhal Ltd,
Park House, 1 Russell Gardens,
London NW11 9NN

Published and distributed in the
United States of America and Canada by the
Naval Institute Press,
291 Wood Road, Annapolis,
Maryland 21402-5034

Library of Congress Control Number: 2005929980

ISBN 1-59114-813-8

Drawings by Veres László
All uncredited photographs from the collection of David Clement
Designed and typeset by Roger Daniels

Printed and bound in Singapore

For Guy

With special thanks to Malcolm Darch, David Clement, George Hogg and the staff of the library at National Maritime Museum Cornwall, and finally to Christopher Monk for his enthusiastic searching.

Contents

Introduction

On 7 February 2005 Ellen MacArthur sailed into the record books with the fastest single-handed circum-navigation ever: 71 days, 14 hours, 18 minutes, and 33 seconds. Throughout the voyage her progress had been charted, followed, and scrutinized by millions, all over the world; at no point were her whereabouts unknown; not once did a change of direction or speed go unnoticed. She experienced only one mishap that seriously threatened the pursuit of the challenge: not the loss of a sail or mast, but the malfunction of the generator, without which she would lose communication with the outside world and her ability to make crucial decisions based not on what *was* happening but on what was *going* to happen. It was a far cry from the ocean voyaging of the past. And yet, the essence of her trip – the ability to power a vessel through the water by using wind – would have been familiar to peoples around the world and through the ages.

Of course, for most sailors of the past MacArthur's high-tech trimaran would be far from familiar (see photo, page 53). Yet on closer inspection they would understand the basic physics of the rig and sail plan. Furthermore, for the likes of the Polynesian sailors, inland Dutch navigators, and some coastal fishermen of colonial America, the rig – if not its size – would be instantly recognizable. But what is that rig? How should it be described? Single-masted with multiple headsails, perhaps a cutter. But with no more than one headsail being set at one time, surely a sloop? Does it matter? Well, it matters if you wish to describe the boat to someone who hasn't seen it, and it matters because the choice of rig has been determined through the course of centuries; surely we owe it to those past seafarers to know what they did and why.

Technological advance in any field stems from a basis of need and is constrained by development – or lack of – in other related technologies. For example, you cannot step a tall single-piece mast on a narrow hull if you don't have the material, such as wire, to support it; nor can you efficiently raise a single sail that is more than twice your body weight – as Ellen MacArthur did – until you have a hoisting system capable of doing most of the work for you.

This book, brief as it is, does not cover the entire historical or regional range of sail plans, but rather considers the arrangements of rigs from the 250-year era of post seventeenth-century 'Western' sail, and highlights the whys and wherefores of choice and change. It is perhaps obvious to say that what suits one sailor in one trade may not – almost certainly will not – suit another sailor in a different trade. Furthermore, what suits today's purpose might not, because of a change in law or economics, suit tomorrow's.

To take specific examples: Polynesian sailors sailed from island to island and often over great distances, but load bearing was secondary to the ability to sail swiftly, often close to shore, and through the shoal waters of coral reefs with small crews. Their craft were light and fast, could sail efficiently in open water but, with fore-and-aft sail plans, were able to manoeuvre in and out of bays, on and off beaches, and make the most of variable coastal winds. Conversely, the great ocean-going cargo carriers of the nineteenth century covered vast distances between ports, transporting massive loads; they spent only a fraction of their time negotiating the confines of port. Thus, the powerful full-rig sail plan – square sails on multiple masts with a small percentage of fore-and-aft sail area – was used to full advantage.

As well as needing to meet the requirements of role, choice of rig will be heavily influenced by the economy of labour. The Polynesian's voyaging vessel had to be suitable for a small crew: island populations were not large and men's lives were not cheap. On the other hand, in the expanding Western World of the eighteenth and early nineteenth centuries manpower was probably the cheapest commodity and shipowners could afford to employ large crews. However, as the century progressed and profits were harder to come by, owners cut back on crews, and rigs changed accordingly: square sails were replaced by fore-and-aft; the full-rigged ship was converted to or replaced by the barque, barquentine, or schooner; masts were reduced in height; machinery was adopted to take the place of men. Throughout, the external influences of contemporary social economics and politics are paramount and to look at the shifting evolution of commercial (and naval) rigs in the West is to trace the history of science, engineering, trade, demographics, and more.

There are, of course, existing books that define rig plans and describe the benefits or uses of specific arrangements – the work of Harold Underhill jumps to mind. But more often than not the authors of such texts were writing in a time when working sail was, if not still in existence, only recently past – memories were sharp and many readers had direct contact with men who 'were there'. Today's readers are less fortunate; it is, after all, half a century since Western commercial sail – in anything other than tourism or education – came to a quiet end. Thus, this book is for the new enthusiast: perhaps a Patrick O'Brian reader, or someone about to sign on for a passage on a square-rigger, or an intrigued visitor to a 'tall-ships' or classic-boat gathering. It seeks to define; reveal some of the subtle differences; look briefly at the outside influences that led to the initial development and ultimate demise of any one of the rigs considered. It does not assume an in-depth knowledge of terminology, but does expect a keen interest. Inevitably some readers will find gaps and will point to rigs not included and to them I apologize and can only say that I have included those rigs that were most common through the age of working sail – both in large ocean-going vessels and in small coastal traders and fishing boats.

And so to return to Ellen MacArthur and her trimaran. Perhaps it's not enough to be able to describe her sail plan as a bermudan sloop, perhaps we should also aspire to understanding why that particular rig was chosen: for a single-handed sailor intent on speed with a relatively light vessel, the rig offers simplicity, close-windedness, light weight, and thanks to modern technology can be shortened, trimmed, or otherwise adjusted quickly and efficiently by a lone person. This book may not present all the answers to all the questions but it will, I hope, lay the foundations upon which further knowledge may be built.

THE SQUARE RIG

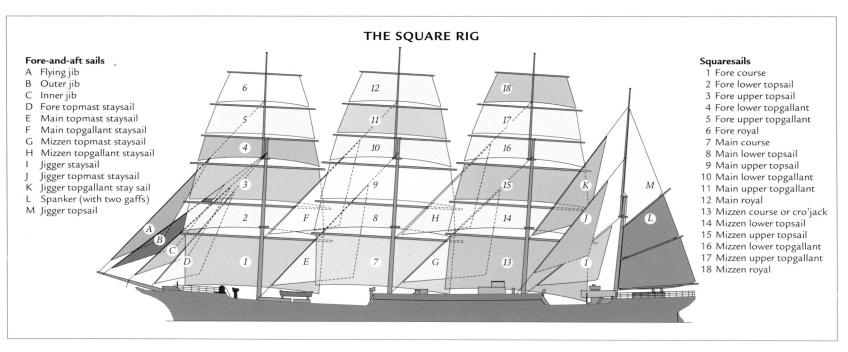

Fore-and-aft sails
A Flying jib
B Outer jib
C Inner jib
D Fore topmast staysail
E Main topmast staysail
F Main topgallant staysail
G Mizzen topmast staysail
H Mizzen topgallant staysail
I Jigger staysail
J Jigger topmast staysail
K Jigger topgallant stay sail
L Spanker (with two gaffs)
M Jigger topsail

Squaresails
1 Fore course
2 Fore lower topsail
3 Fore upper topsail
4 Fore lower topgallant
5 Fore upper topgallant
6 Fore royal
7 Main course
8 Main lower topsail
9 Main upper topsail
10 Main lower topgallant
11 Main upper topgallant
12 Main royal
13 Mizzen course or cro'jack
14 Mizzen lower topsail
15 Mizzen upper topsail
16 Mizzen lower topgallant
17 Mizzen upper topgallant
18 Mizzen royal

THE FORE-AND-AFT RIG

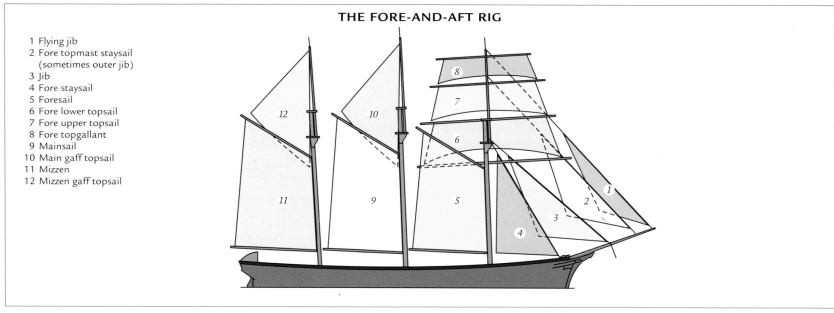

1 Flying jib
2 Fore topmast staysail
  (sometimes outer jib)
3 Jib
4 Fore staysail
5 Foresail
6 Fore lower topsail
7 Fore upper topsail
8 Fore topgallant
9 Mainsail
10 Main gaff topsail
11 Mizzen
12 Mizzen gaff topsail

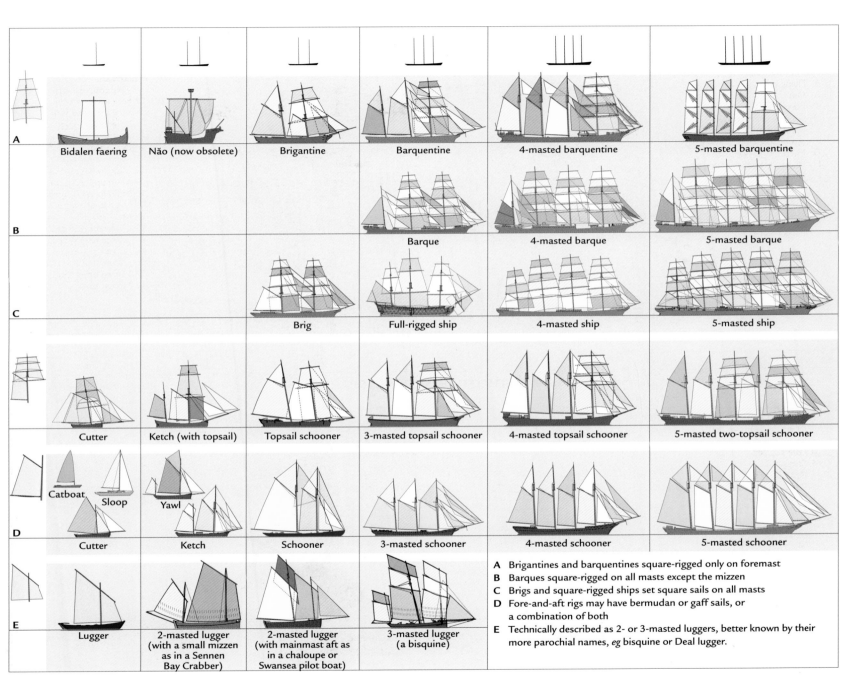

A

Bidalen faering | Não (now obsolete) | Brigantine | Barquentine | 4-masted barquentine | 5-masted barquentine

B

Barque | 4-masted barque | 5-masted barque

C

Brig | Full-rigged ship | 4-masted ship | 5-masted ship

D

Cutter | Ketch (with topsail) | Topsail schooner | 3-masted topsail schooner | 4-masted topsail schooner | 5-masted two-topsail schooner

Catboat, Sloop

Yawl

Cutter | Ketch | Schooner | 3-masted schooner | 4-masted schooner | 5-masted schooner

E

Lugger | 2-masted lugger (with a small mizzen as in a Sennen Bay Crabber) | 2-masted lugger (with mainmast aft as in a chaloupe or Swansea pilot boat) | 3-masted lugger (a bisquine)

A Brigantines and barquentines square-rigged only on foremast
B Barques square-rigged on all masts except the mizzen
C Brigs and square-rigged ships set square sails on all masts
D Fore-and-aft rigs may have bermudan or gaff sails, or a combination of both
E Technically described as 2- or 3-masted luggers, better known by their more parochial names, *eg* bisquine or Deal lugger.

CHAPTER

1

The Full-rigged Ship

``The full-rigged ship is probably longer lasting than any other type, going back some 500 years, to the mid 1500s. For sheer power and speed over long distance, no rig could outclass it and at the height of its development it attained ocean-going records that stood unchallenged until the appearance of high-tech racing yachts in the late twentieth century.

DEFINITION

The full-rigged ship carries three or more masts, all of which are square-rigged. Each mast is in at least three parts: lower, top, and topgallant; and usually in four: the highest section being the royal (although in later ships the topgallant and royal masts were combined in a single pole mast). Fore-and-aft sails are carried on stays running forward from the masts, and a gaff-rigged spanker is set on the mast nearest the stern (the mizzen on a three-master).

The squaresails are named according to the mast on which their yards are crossed; thus the main lower topsail, for example, is the lower of two topsails bent on yards crossed on the main topmast. On each mast the fully-developed ship carries (from the deck up): course (on the mizzen this sail is known as either the 'mizzen sail' or the 'cross-jack'; on the main as either the 'main course' or 'mainsail'; on the fore, the 'fore course' or 'foresail', etc), topsail (lower and upper), topgallant (lower and upper), royal; less common are the skysail, moonsail, and, most rare, the star grazer. From time to time one even hears of a tiny square-sail being set above the star grazer: called an 'angel's footstool', it is probably fictional. Fore-and-aft sails include jibs and staysails – the latter being named according to the stay on which they are set; the spanker, usually gaff rigged; and spencers, not always carried, but sometimes set abaft the main- and foremasts in the manner of the spanker.

THE DEVELOPMENT OF THE SQUARE SAIL

1 The earliest predominantly square-rigged vessel of size was the south-European *não* of about 1450. The hull is a recognisable early version of the ships of the next three centuries.

2 A *caravela redonda* of the late 1400s, as used by Columbus for his voyages of exploration.

3 The Portuguese *Santa Caterina de Monte Sinai* of 1520 – note the appearance of topsails on the fore- and mainmasts, and the spritsail.

4 *Vasa* of Sweden, 1628, now has topsails and topgallants, a square topsail on the mizzen, and two spritsails.

5 HMS *Victory* of 1765 displays all the ingredients of the 'modern' full-rigged

ship with a large gaff-rigged spanker, three-sectioned masts, and fore-and-aft staysails.

1 2 3 4 5

A nineteenth-century full-rigged three-decker at anchor in Portsmouth. With no sails bent on it is possible to see clearly the doubling of the three-section masts; in comparison to contemporary merchant ships her squaresails were massive, requiring a huge crew to handle them.

Extra, lightwind 'flying' sails include studdingsails (pronounced stuns'ls), set on booms extending outboard of the principal top, topgallant, and royal yards; a ringtail set like a studding sail abaft the spanker; and watersails set beneath the boom of the spanker, spencers, and lower studdingsails. Flying sails were only set in a following wind in relatively calm weather.

HISTORY

The history of the full-rigged ship is really the 'modern' history of square rig. Squaresails are the earliest of all sails, seen on ancient Egyptian and Roman vessels set on short masts for downwind sailing. It was probably the Scandinavians who first discovered that by bracing the yard so that the sail was set at an angle, a vessel could be sailed upwind as well as down.

The Scandanavian, or northern, tradition developed the single-masted, square-rigged, clinkerbuilt cog, the most important trading vessel of the Middle Ages. The Mediterranean, or southern, tradition of frame-first construction combined with lateen sails, is seen clearly in the caravel, from where the term 'carvel' originated. Sometime in the fifteenth century – where, when, and how is not known – the process began whereby these two traditions merged,

THE NORDIC SQUARESAIL

The Viking trading and raiding ships of 1,000 years ago were powered by a single squaresail bent to a yard crossed on a stout mast stepped directly on to the keel slightly forward of amidships. On larger vessels the mast was supported by multiple shrouds led aft and to windward of the sail, a single forestay to the stemhead, and often a backstay to the top of the sternpost. The smaller the vessel – Viking sailing craft ranged from small one-man inshore boats to longships of 100ft or more – the less complicated was the running rigging, but at its most sophisticated the Viking sail had multiple lines from its edges to flatten and control the set, as well as lines from the clew and tack for hauling in and tacking down; there were also sheets from the yard arms to control their angle to the wind; the yard could be set almost parallel to the vessel's centreline, thus enabling fair windward performance.

While the Vikings did not survive into the modern era their sailing influences can still be seen in the small craft of the Norwegian fjords. The faerings, for example, although essentially rowing boats, carried a sail for auxiliary power. Originally the rig was always a squaresail set on a mast stepped amidships; the sail was tacked down to the gunwale and controlled by two sheets, a clewline, a running line from the middle of the sail, and a downhaul so that the sail could be quickly lowered. The mast was supported by a single forestay and two pairs of shrouds. It was a relatively complicated rig for a small oared boat and in parts of Norway was replaced during the 1800s by either a dipping lugsail or a spritsail-and-jib arrangement.

Further afield there is evidence of a Viking her-

ABOVE *Norge*, an example of a later Norwegian coastal cargo vessel, a Nordlandsfarer, with large square sail and small topsail – a rig remarkably like that of the Humber keel (see p.13). The mainsail appears to have bonnets attached to its foot – or perhaps a single bonnet of two panels.

itage in the islands of Scotland – the Fair Isle yole carried a true squaresail, while the Ness yole set a dipping squaresail that was passed forward of the mast when tacking – it was carried outside the standing rigging in squaresail fashion.

In recent years the staff of the Viking Ship Museum in Roskilde, Denmark, has led the world in researching the sails, rigging, and performance of Viking vessels through highly accurate replicas based on wrecks excavated from the Roskilde fjord.

ABOVE Often though quite primitive the traditional Norwegian squaresail was in fact remarkably sophisticated, as can be seen on this reconstruction, *Saga Sigler* sailing in Lerwick Harbour, Shetland, June 1984. Note the multiple lines leading not only from the sail's edges and yard, but also from the but – all were designed to help flatten and control the set of the sail. (Shetland Museum)

ABOVE This model of a Ness Yole, housed in the Shetland Museum, shows the remarkable similarity between its rig and that of its Viking ancestors. However, this sail, while almost square, is a dipping lugsail. Note the shroud to leeward; when tacked the sail will be dipped forward of the mast and be set on the new leeward side outboard of the shroud, which will not have been unfastened. (Shetland Museum)

and the squaresail and lateen were combined; perhaps the lateen mizzen was added to aid manoeuvrability. The Catalan *não* represents the beginning of the process that led to the full-rigged ship and by the late fifteenth century the carrack had emerged, a type of ship that facilitated extensive ocean exploration and worldwide trade. It was the greatest breakthrough in the evolution of the ship and became the established form right down to the great clippers of the nineteenth century.

Carracks were typically three- or four-masted and carried two or three squaresails on the fore- and mainmasts, a spritsail beneath the bowsprit, and lateen sails on the mizzens (the aftermost mast being known as the bonaventure mizzen). Early famous examples of this rig were Henry VIII's great warships *Mary Rose*, built in 1510, and *Henri Grace à Dieu* of 1514.

Cutty Sark, a late example of the extreme clipper, had a tall rig: her mainmast, consisting of lower, top, topgallant, and royal masts, was 145ft 9in from deck to truck. But it was also a wide sail plan: the main and foreyards were 78ft long – the ship's beam was only 36ft.

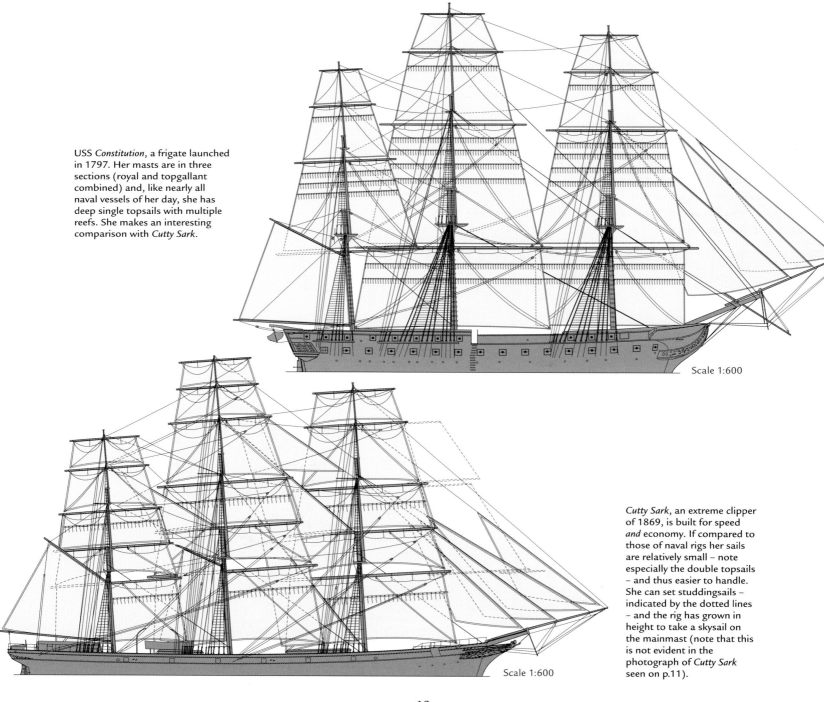

USS *Constitution*, a frigate launched in 1797. Her masts are in three sections (royal and topgallant combined) and, like nearly all naval vessels of her day, she has deep single topsails with multiple reefs. She makes an interesting comparison with *Cutty Sark*.

Scale 1:600

Cutty Sark, an extreme clipper of 1869, is built for speed *and* economy. If compared to those of naval rigs her sails are relatively small – note especially the double topsails – and thus easier to handle. She can set studdingsails – indicated by the dotted lines – and the rig has grown in height to take a skysail on the mainmast (note that this is not evident in the photograph of *Cutty Sark* seen on p.11).

Scale 1:600

THE HUMBER KEEL

For more than 500 years cargoes were carried on the inland waterways of north-east England by Humber keels. Flat-bottomed barges their later dimensions were determined by the sizes of locks through which they had to navigate, but typically they ranged in length from 58ft to 68ft and in beam from 15ft to 16ft. The rig was a single mast stepped forward of amidships supported by a pair of shrouds on either side and a single forestay, which was used in conjunction with a windlass to raise and lower the mast (with all sail standing) in order to navigate beneath bridges. A deep squaresail was set from the main yard and, in fine weather, a small square topsail was set from the masthead.

The type came into its own during the industrialisation of the northeast when the canal and river networks of Yorkshire, Lincolnshire, and Nottinghamshire allowed the keels to sail far inland, while their robust construction and deep lee-boards helped them withstand the strong currents and short seas of the Humber estuary. Like the Thames barges to the south (see p.64), the Humber keels were the pre-railway vehicles of choice for the rapid transportation of bulk cargoes. They remained in trade until the twentieth century but in the earliest decades of the 1900s their number fell steadily until grants were made available from 1939 to convert any keel still sailing to motor.

Today there is one Humber keel operated under sail: the 61ft 6in *Comrade* was iron-built in 1923, motorised in 1933, de-rigged in 1942, and reconverted to the traditional sailing rig by the Humber Keel and Sloop Preservation Society in 1976.

A small fleet of Humber keels makes the most of a light breeze. The one to the far right of the picture has a block above the yard, perhaps for raising a small topsail – certainly all would commonly have had topsails. None of the four appears to be much laden.

Inevitably it was the development of fighting navies that influenced the early evolution of larger ships and their rigging. Most attention was devoted to hull form and size, and early treatises concentrate little on sail plans or rigging requirements. Nevertheless, rigs did continue to develop. By the mid 1600s bonaventure mizzens had disappeared and staysails were being introduced; by the end of the century jibs were being used in conjunction with and, in some instances replacing, the spritsails; and by the middle of the 1700s the lateen mizzen was being superseded by the gaff-rigged spanker with topsail and topgallant. (Thought to have originated on small craft in Scandinavian and Dutch regions the gaff trysail most probably replaced the sprit or lateen mizzen on full-rigged ships as the vessels became larger and the spars associated with the earlier sails became too cumbersome. Britain's Royal Navy did not fully abandon the lateen yard until the 1790s although on merchant ships it had almost totally faded out by the mid 1770s.)

By the end of the 1700s the Royal Navy had adopted many of the final developments of full-rig sailplans in their ships of the line and frigates. The full rig was immensely suitable for a warship: it was powerful enough to carry the great size and weight of hull needed to accommodate guns and men, fast enough to give chase, and, once engaged in a broadside action, its lack of swift manoeuvrability was of little importance. A typical First Rate ship of the Napoleonic era was Nelson's flagship, *Victory*, in which he commanded the fleet against the French at Trafalgar in 1805. Although launched in 1765, by the turn of the century *Victory* had a completely modernised rig. Three-masted, she had a large gaff-rig spanker, whose loose foot was clewed to a boom that overhung the stern; the main- and foremasts each carried a course, single topsail, single topgallant, and royal, while on the mizzen she set a single topsail and topgallant above the spanker; beneath the bowsprit in light airs she set a spritsail and sprit topsail. With the exception of the royals, all the squaresails on the fore- and mainmasts could be extended by studdingsails,

OPPOSITE 'Outward Bound Ship Under Full Sail' by Eduardo Frederico de Martino, 1882.
A four-masted full-rig ship ghosts along on a calm day. On her two taller masts – main and mizzen – she has a course, lower and upper topsails, lower and upper topgallants, and a royal. On the fore and mizzen masts she has single topgallant sails.
(Royal Exchange Art Gallery, London)

and all the topsails, topgallants, and courses could be reefed in heavy weather.

On all full-rig ships of the late 1700s the stays led forward from mast to mast, which introduced a sometimes disastrous interdependence: one falling mast could bring the others with it. The bowsprit was supported by the bobstay running down to the stem while the jibboom and flying jibboom were stayed to the dolphin striker. This evocatively named spar was first introduced in the mid 1700s: as headsails became more important and powerful the bowsprit required more efficient staying to counteract the lifting power of the canvas; nearly all large modern vessels were fitted with dolphin strikers (to spread and tension the sprit stays) by the end of the century. Where the squaresails gave the ship power, it was the fore-and-aft sails that provided manoeuvrability. On *Victory* the mizzenmast had three staysails, the mainmast four, and the foremast four headsails.

Naval ships of the mid to late 1700s used for carrying troops or stores, display smaller rigs. Their crews were smaller, speed less critical, and a smaller rig was safer and more easily handled.

As naval ships were developing and evolving so, too, were merchant ships. Before the sixteenth century merchant ships were typically small and employed in local trading but with the discovery and exploration of the Americas in the late fifteenth and early sixteenth centuries, and the opening up of trade routes to the East in the late sixteenth

The 250ft iron-hulled *Loch Vennacher*, built in Glasgow, Scotland, in 1875, is a beautifully proportioned ship with her sleek lines, raked masts, and generous sail plan – although many contemporary Clyde-built ships had loftier rigs with double topgallants (rather than the singles seen here) and skysails above the royals.

Scale 1:750

ABOVE *Preussen* had a total of forty-seven sails – courses, double topsails, double topgallants, royals, staysails, jibs, *and* the double gaff-rigged spanker (not set in this drawing).

RIGHT *Preussen* was the first – and until the twenty-first century – only five-masted full-rigged ship. She was 407ft 10in long and had 35,424ft of standing rigging and 102,303ft of running rigging in wire, hemp, rope, and chain. Launched in 1902 she drove ashore just east of Dover in 1910, after a collision with a steamer, whose skipper was said to have underestimated her speed.

BELOW *Royal Clipper*, the largest full-rig ship sailing today and the only five-masted ship to be built since *Preussen* (see p.17). At 439ft LOA, she sets forty-two sails on a comparatively short rig (nothing above the topgallants), and has accommodations for 227 'guests'.

County of Peebles was the first commercial four-masted full-rigged ship (although *L'Invention* was perhaps the first example of the type, launched seventy-four years earlier in 1801). All four masts were in four sections. Note the single topsail on the jigger mast.

century, larger, more powerful ocean-going ships were needed. Through the seventeenth, eighteenth, and nineteenth centuries ships went further and further afield and for more and more varied cargoes – commercial competition arrived and with it came the importance of both time and capacity relative to profit.

By the mid 1800s the full-rigged ship's sail plan had become the archetypal 'modern-day' image of the type: three masts, square-rigged on all, with as many as seven sails to a single mast. As new industrial technologies swept through onshore trades, so their effects were seen in ship rigs. Wire rope, first used in railways, mining, and then telegraphy, allowed for taller masts and reduced windage. In the 1850s it was calculated that wire rigging was a quarter the bulk and half the weight of same-strength hemp. Thus, a ship with wire standing rigging could retain a tall sail plan but had enhanced stability thanks to reduced weight aloft. By 1857 75 per cent of all ships being fitted out in Liverpool, England, were rigged with wire rope. With

HM Bark *Endeavour*, a modern, accurate replica of Captain James Cook's ship of discovery – the 'bark' of her title refers to her hull shape rather than her rig, which is a typical naval full-ship rig of the late eighteenth century. (Jenny Bennett)

The steel-hulled ship *Port Logan*, built by Russell & Co. in 1895. Handsomely proportioned she carries a tall but conventional rig of course, double topsails, single topgallant, and royal on all three masts.

such technology came greater options. The immediate development was for rigs to become taller but, by the mid 1870s, there was a new vogue for four-masted ships, which spread the sail more evenly along a longer hull, and offered more versatility when it came to reducing sail – the aftermost mast was known as the jigger.

Despite the development of steam power, sail continued to rule in merchant shipping during the 1800s. The dis-tances travelled were immense – from Shanghai to Beachy Head with tea; from Sydney to London with wool; from New York to San Francisco via Cape Horn for gold – and for most of the century the technology of steam at sea was neither sufficiently reliable nor cost effective to be viable over great distances.

Locally and inshore the steamer made significant inroads but on the world's oceans the great merchant ships of the

1800s were the clippers – a term that referred to hull-shape rather than rig; indeed, clippers could be anything from full-rigged ships to schooners (see p.73). They were cargo-carrying ships whose ultimate aim was to be fast; and to be fast they needed a large sail area. For this the full-rigged ship was ideal.

A typical late example, the 213ft, 921-registered-tons *Cutty Sark* (now famous principally because she is the last survivor) was launched in 1869 for the China tea trade and had a greater sail area than any other ship in the trade at that time. Her rig was tall: the mainmast was 145ft 9in from deck to truck and consisted of a lower mast, topmast, topgallant mast, royal mast, and skysail mast; it was also broad: the main- and foreyards were both 78ft long – 42ft more than the ship's beam. For her size the sail area was immense: 32,000sq.ft. And she was a fast ship: in 1870 her first voyage back from China was made in 109 days. However, even before she had begun in the tea trade the viability of sail to the East was threatened by the opening of the Suez Canal, and in later life *Cutty Sark* entered the Australian wool trade for which her sail plan was reduced in order to contend with rounding Cape Horn. She remained fast, however, and in 1877–78 sailed from Newcastle, New South Wales, to the Lizard, Cornwall, in 69 days.

Launched in 1851 the 225ft, 1,139-ton *Flying Cloud* was built for the California gold-rush trade. Her rig was also tall: the three-sectioned mainmast stood 127ft above deck (on all three masts her topgallant poles carried lower and upper topgallants and a royal). At 25,655sq.ft her maximum sail area was not enormous but, when built, she was the largest American clipper to date and claimed many speed records: when most ships were averaging 100 days from New York to San Francisco *Flying Cloud* set a new record of 89 days 21 hours in 1851 and broke it by 13 hours in 1854 (her record stood until broken by the high-performance yacht *Thursday's Child*, sailing the route in 80 days in 1989).

The French ship *L'Invention*, launched in 1801, is thought to have been the first example of a four-masted full-rigged ship, but the type really became popular in the 1870s. Of several ships named *County of...* built for the Craig line, *County of Peebles* was the first commercial four-master. Launched in 1875 she was 266ft 7in long, 38ft 9in beam, and 1,614 net tons. Her four masts were in three sections but she carried no sails above the royals and only single topgallants; the jigger had a single topsail.

Until the beginning of the twenty-first century, when the five-masted full-rigged cruise liner, *Royal Clipper,* was launched for the Star Clipper line, the only five-masted full-rigged ship was *Preussen*, built in Geestemunde, Germany, in 1902. Working in the nitrate trade, she was a large ship: 407ft 10in long, 53ft 6in beam, and 5,081 tons. Both her hull and spars were in steel and, typically of that time, her masts were in two parts: lower and topmast combined, topgallant and royal combined. She crossed six yards (ie carried six squaresails) on all five masts and had a total sail area of about 50,000sq.ft in 47 sails.

The opening of the Suez Canal (1869) was not the only threat to commercial sailing routes – in the same year, the completion of the transcontinental railway from the east to the west coast of America caused a dramatic and almost immediate decline in sailing ships making passage for San Francisco. The last, most sustainable trade for the full-rigged ship was in nitrate from the west coast of South America; steamships were still unsuitable for rounding Cape Horn, but when the Panama Canal was opened in 1914, this trade, too, was infiltrated by the steamers.

In their time, the great full-rigged ships had achieved some extraordinary feats and established remarkable records but by the 1920s they had had their day. Some did continue in trade, most notably the iron, steel, and wooden ships bought at unimaginably low prices by Gustaf Erikson of Åland in the early 1900s. For the most part, however, sailing trades returned to being local, and with rising employment costs forcing ships to run with ever decreasing crews, smaller, more manoeuvrable sailing ships once again came to the fore.

Today the full rig is popular among sail-training fleets on both new builds and ex-merchant ships as it requires a large crew and thus gives optimum opportunity to cadets.

CHAPTER 2

The Barque

In the later years of commercial sail the barque became as popular and, latterly, superseded the full-rigged ship in the ocean trade. Its rig was easier to handle, cheaper to maintain and, though less powerful than the full rig, allowed shipowners to reduce crew sizes and maintain profits.

DEFINITION

The barque carries three, four, or five masts, square-rigged on all but the aftermost. The nomenclature of sails, masts, and yards is as seen in the full-rigged ship (see p.6). In most barques the spanker is a single fore-and-aft, four-cornered gaff sail, but variations include the jib-headed (or leg o'mutton) spanker popular in America, and the German double-gaff spanker (easy to furl and reef and also sets flat by virtue of each gaff having its own vang).

As a development rig there were, inevitably, variations in the barque. The rig's definition could be further subdivided beyond the number of masts stepped. In Britain there were terms such as 'English Rig': on the square-rigged masts the topgallants were singles rather than doubles and there were royals above; the 'Scottish Rig': similar to the English Rig but with a jib-headed spanker. And within such broader categories there were also more precise definitions, the most common being the stump-topgallant or bald-headed rig, which did away with royals and skysails and became increasingly popular for its easier handling.

1 *Great Republic*, a four-masted barque of 1853, was the largest wooden sailing vessel ever built – 352ft LOA. Her jigger is relatively small, set well aft, and has a pronounced rake.
2 *R.P. Rithet* of 1892 is of particular interest for her jib-headed spanker.
3 *France II* of 1911 was the largest ever sailing ship – 418ft LOA and 5,633 tons. Without royals her rig is unexceptional but practical.
4 One of the last large commercial sailing ships, *Magdalene Vinnen* of 1921. Her rig has the 'normal' double topsails, double topgallants, royals, and staysails, although the pole lower-topmasts on the square masts are of interest, as are the typically German twin gaffs on the spanker.
5 *Tenacious* was built as a sail-training ship for the British Jubilee Sailing Trust in 2000. Her rig is conventional although it is interesting to note the modern polemasts and the 'German' double-gaffed spanker.

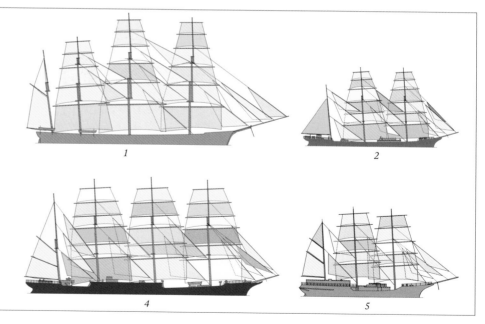

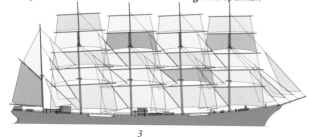

Originally called *Padua* the now-Russian-owned barque *Kruzenstern*, is the largest vessel in today's sail-training fleets. Built in Germany in 1926 she crosses skysail yards on all three square masts, and has the typically German double-gaff spanker. (David Kaye)

The term 'jackass' is often linked with the barque rig and was used to describe any barque that deviated from the norm. For instance, a four-masted barque carrying all square on the fore and main but all fore-and-aft on the mizzen and jigger was a 'jackass barque'; so, too, was a three-master with all square on the fore, square topsails and topgallants above a fore-and-aft main course, and all fore-and-aft on the mizzen. Jackass bar-ques were also known as 'hermaphrodite barques' and, in the case of the three-masters, sometimes as 'Jack barquentines'; in America a four-masted jackass barque might also be called a 'shipentine'. Other departures included the polacca barque whose masts were in one piece and set a combination of fore-and-aft below and square above on all but the aftermost mast, which was entirely fore-and-aft.

HISTORY

In eighteenth-century Britain the term 'bark' referred not to rig but to hull form – generally small, often bluff-bowed, full-bodied, and relatively flat-bottomed. Such vessels were used for local bulk-cargo carrying and were often adopted by the Royal Navy for use in exploration (a typical example was Captain James Cook's first command, HM Bark *Endeavour*, built as a Whitby cat in 1765 and full-rigged). However, in the early nineteenth century the term 'barque' (borrowed from the French) had come to refer to rig and the definition by hull shape was largely forgotten. (It should be noted that in North America the continued modern use of the word 'bark' refers to rig.)

The first known reference to a barque – as a rig definition – is in Falconer's 1769 *A Universal Dictionary of the Marine*. But the type gained popularity from the 1830s onward, and most especially in the second half of the nineteenth century. There were two principal reasons for its development: shipbuilders looked to enlarging the two-masted brig (see p.38) and added an additional mast to expand the sail plan; and, more typically from the 1850s, it became the popular alternative to the full rig as it allowed for a reduction in crew size without compromising efficiency – it took the full-rigged sail plan and, for ease of handling, removed the yards on the aftermost mast; then, to make up for the reduced sail area, added a fore-and-aft topsail above the spanker.

Never as powerful as the full rig, in its early days the barque found favour in local trades and in those ocean trades where speed was not the prime consideration. As steam-powered shipping increasingly encroached on commercial shipping, sailing-ship designers concentrated on capacity for bulk-carrying rather than fine lines for fast passages. But even on those routes still suited to sail, shipowners had to fight to hold their own: costs had to be cut and the easiest option was to reduce crew sizes. The fore-and-aft sail requires fewer men to handle it and, an added bonus, needs less running rigging. But there was a reluctance to forego the sheer power of the square rig and

LEFT The four-masted barque *Archibald Russell* carried identical yards and gear on all her squaresailed masts – thus at times of breakage or maintenance, gear was interchangeable. Launched in 1905 *Archibald Russell* was the last large sailing merchant ship for British owners.

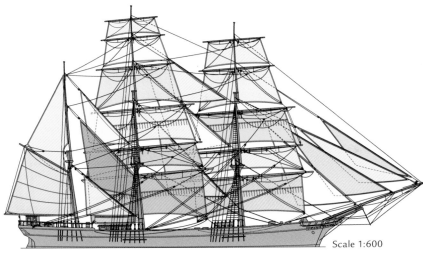

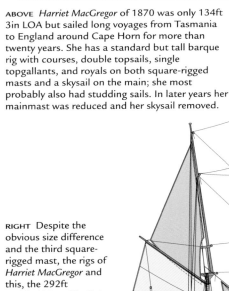

thus a compromise, the barque, came into its own. Hundreds were built throughout the Western World and they became the great survivors of the squaresail era. In Scandinavia many small examples were built for the coastal and Baltic trades, while in Britain, America, and Canada larger ones were commissioned for ocean routes.

But even as the barque was coming to dominate commercial sail so it continued to evolve. Forever looking to maximise profits, shipowners and builders sought ways to reduce costs without compromising efficiency. The most dramatic and obvious of all such adaptations was the stump-topgallant or baldheaded rig. The height of the sail plan was lowered on the square-rigged masts and no sail was set above the upper topgallants. However, this caused a sizeable reduction in sail area and so the yards were

ABOVE *Harriet MacGregor* of 1870 was only 134ft 3in LOA but sailed long voyages from Tasmania to England around Cape Horn for more than twenty years. She has a standard but tall barque rig with courses, double topsails, single topgallants, and royals on both square-rigged masts and a skysail on the main; she most probably also had studding sails. In later years her mainmast was reduced and her skysail removed.

RIGHT Despite the obvious size difference and the third square-rigged mast, the rigs of *Harriet MacGregor* and this, the 292ft *Archibald Russell* built in 1905, are remarkably similar although that of the later vessel is relatively lower and, with all square-rigged masts being equal in height and gear the yards and fittings were interchangeable.

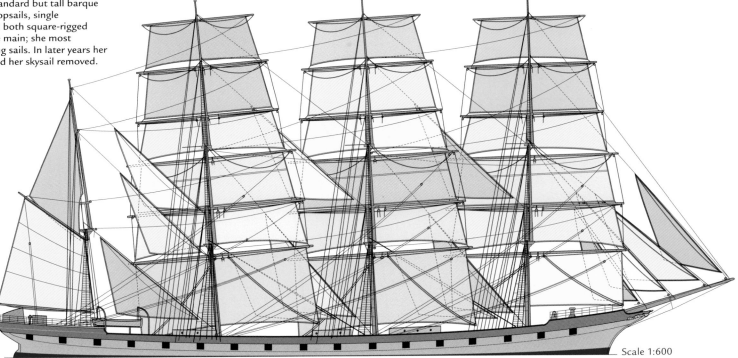

Scale 1:600

LEFT The four-masted barque *Lawhill* was unusual in having her topgallant masts rigged abaft the topmasts – this was perhaps not as attractive as the more conventional arrangement but did mean that a topgallant mast could be sent down without affecting the yards below.

RIGHT The French auxiliary barque *Charles Gounod* is rigged 'jubilee fashion'; no royals above the double-topsails and topgallants. She was captured and sunk by a German Imperial Navy ship in mid Atlantic in 1917.

LEFT Manned by a crew of twenty-eight men, the four-masted barque *Pommern* was launched as *Mneme* in 1903. She had no royals and her lower and topmasts were in one piece – pole masts. She survives as a museum ship, with her original arrangement, moored alongside in Mariehamn, Åland.

Ruth, a conventional barque with double topsails, single topgallants, and royals. A Cardiff pilot cutter is tied astern, its mainsail partially triced up – it is interesting to note that even with this reduced power the cutter is not falling back on the line.

lengthened – the result was a large sail plan that required less running and standing rigging, and so reduced costs. Sadly, the rig lacked the elegance of the earlier full rig whose sail plans tapered as they rose.

Technological development further affected the aesthetics of the barque rig. As the fore-and-aft spanker grew in importance so did the height of the mizzen mast itself until, to quote Harold Underhill, it created a mast 'that in the eyes of the traditionalists did not belong but rather dominated the rig'. By the late nineteenth century sails had grown to almost excessive widths: whereas in the middle of the century the royal would be roughly as deep as it was wide at its head, by the end of the 1800s it could be three times as wide. Pole (rather than fidded) lower and topmasts had also become common, giving square-rigged masts an unfamiliar 'bare' look. Finally, one of the most practical if, again, not wholly attractive, later developments was in making a barque's square-rigged masts and spars identical so that all yards, gear, and sails above the courses were interchangeable.

There have been many famous barques. The largest was the largest sailing ship ever built: the great steel-hulled auxiliary five-master, *France II,* launched in 1911. She was 5,806 tons and carried the typical baldheaded rig of the day with pole topmasts, and a driver (the fifth mast) that was a single pole from keel to truck. Smaller by far, but perhaps of equal fame, was the diminutive *Harriet McGregor.* Built in Hobart, Tasmania, in 1870, she was of wood construction: 331 tons, 134ft 3in long, 27ft 6in beam, and 15ft 11in depth of hold. For twenty-four years she made round trips from Hobart to London via Cape Horn (averaging seven months including a five-week layover in London) leaving in December and returning in July when she would load cargo and set sail for Mauritius, return with more cargo to Hobart, refit, reload, and set off again for London. She carried a tall rig with double topsails, single topgallants, royals, and a skysail on the main. She was said to be lively and wet in heavy weather, but in her twenty-four years suffered only one fatality – the same could not be said for many vessels ten times her size.

RIGHT The *Earl of Pembroke* was built as a schooner in Sweden in 1948 but was bought by the Square Sail Shipyard of Charlestown, Cornwall, in 1979 and in 1994 was rerigged as a late-eighteenth-century barque with single topsails and topgallants. At 145ft LOA she is 10ft longer than was *Harriet MacGregor* (see p.25) but her rig is considerably smaller. (Dalgleish Images Ltd)

The earliest four-masted barque was the *Great Republic* – the largest wooden sailing ship ever built and, at 4,555 tons, when launched the largest ship ever built in America. She was designed and constructed by Donald McKay of Boston in 1853 and carried a rig of exceptional size. The fore-, main-, and mizzenmasts were conventionally spaced but the jigger was set far back, so that it looked somewhat removed from the rest of the rig. She carried double topsails and, on the fore- and mainmasts, set skysails; her gaff spanker was relatively narrow. (The use of wood for such a large ship was not unusual in North America in the mid 1800s; throughout that century American and Canadian yards continued to build in wood while those in Britain and the rest of Europe began to favour iron and then steel.)

Before the commissioning of sail-training ships in the late 1900s one of the latest barques to be launched in Britain and the last large sailing ship to be ordered by British owners at that time was the *Archibald Russell* (see p.24). Built in 1905 she was entirely typical of the day: steel-hulled, four-masted, with a wide, almost square rig consisting of double topsails, double topgallants, and royals with all the yards and gear of the squaresailed masts being identical.

Barques continue to be favoured in modern sail-

RIGHT Built by Russell & Co of Glasgow in 1903 (two years before the *Archibald Russell* – see p.24), the four-masted barque *Ormsary,* like *Charles Gounod,* was rigged 'jubilee fashion'.

training fleets – many were built for trade and were easily converted, others were built specifically for training. Of the several launched in the second half of the twentieth century: *Gorch Fock II*, a 1,870-ton, 266ft-long, steel-hulled barque, was built in Hamburg for the German Navy in 1958; *Gloria*, 250ft long, was launched in Bilbao, Spain, for the Columbian Navy in 1968; *Kaiwo Maru*, a four-masted steel-hulled barque of 2,556 tons, was launched in Japan in 1989; and most recently *Tenacious*, a wood-hulled, 213ft, three-master of 690 tons, was launched in the UK in 2000 for the Jubilee Sailing Trust to train able-bodied and disabled crews.

ABOVE *Potosi*, built in Geestemunde, Germany, in 1895, was typical of the large German barques of her day, with course, double topsails, double topgallants, and royals on all her squaresailed masts and a double-gaff spanker.

LEFT Built in Glasgow in 1891 the 305ft four-masted *Invertrossachs* was lost in February 1892, just three months after this photograph was taken. Note the common practice of sending down the upper yards to the lowers for stowage – the doublings prevent them from being lowered further. The staysails are hoisted furled with rotten cotton ready for breaking out.

CHAPTER 3

The Barquentine

The barquentine was the last square-rig development in commercial sail. Emerging in the mid 1800s, like the barque it answered an economic need: reduced squaresail was well-suited to small- and medium-sized cargo carriers and called for smaller crews and lower running costs at a time when there was increased competition from power – at sea and on land.

DEFINITION

The barquentine carries three or more masts square-rigged on the foremast alone (which is in three sections: lower, top, topgallant). As with all vessels of multiple masts, from bow to stern the masts are: fore, main, mizzen, jigger, driver, and spanker (even at the height of its popularity it was not common to have more than four masts in British and Euro-pean barquentines but was relatively so in America and Canada – for 6- and 7-masted terminology see p. 76).

Typically, the fore-and-aft sails are large gaff sails with jib-headed topsails above and are set on masts of similar or identical heights. Staysails are set from the main- and foremasts but not, usually, on the after masts. In Britain four-sided staysails between the main and fore were not uncommon from the late 1860s and occasionally a four-sided mizzen topmast staysail would be set instead of a main jib-headed topsail – or in conjunction with a topsail if conditions were favourable.

HISTORY

Although the barquentine was a relatively modern devel-opment, its origins are somewhat mysterious. It was a while

1 The avant-garde *Transit* of 1800 was the first of three experimental ships designed for efficient sailing to windward.
2 *Marmora* is considerably more conventional. Launched in Bath, Maine, 1845, her aft-raked masts are reminiscent of the fast clipper schooners of the early nineteenth century (see p.73), and her overlapping boomless mainsail also suggests schooner influence.
3 *Union*, launched in Scotland, 1867, is typical of the era, with a conventional square-rigged foremast and sizeable fore-and-aft sails on both main and mizzen.
4 A French fisherman of about 1900. Built for working on the Grand Banks she would have made the most of her square sails on the long ocean passages.
5 Shackleton's *Endurance* was built in Norway as *Polaris*. Her sail area is modest and her mainsail is boomless to accommodate the chimney of the all-important auxiliary steam engine.

1

2

3

4

5

before the term 'barquentine' caught on and tracing early examples has proved difficult and often confusing. Documentary evidence of the name first appeared in the 1860s and it would seem that the term, if not the rig itself, originated in America. Possibly the earliest written reference appears in the 1861–63 logbook of the American ship *Cremorne* where mention is made of the 'barkentine' *Fairy*. The term seems to have been in simultaneous early use in Britain – in his diary of 1866 the Glasgow shipbuilder Alexander Stephens noted a quotation for a 'composite three-masted Barkentine'. In 1874 the Lloyd's register includes 'barquentine' in its list of abbreviations, as did the Mercantile Navy List of 1876, although here it was spelt 'barkantine'. However, despite the emergence of the new terminology barquentines continued to be described as three-masted brigantines or schooners well into the 1870s,

Built for the Polish Naval Academy in 1982 *ORP Iskra* sets a gaff mainsail with jib-headed topsail (not seen here), and a jib-headed mizzen, her foremast crosses yards for a course, double topsails, and topgallants. (Nigel Pert)

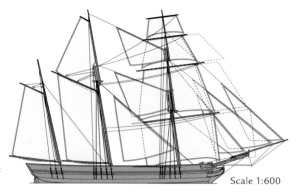

After the *Transits* of 1800–19 (see p.32) *Bonanza* of 1830 was one of the earliest known barquentines. Her masts have a distinct aft rake and her gaff main and mizzen sails are relatively modest. Her foremast is stepped well forward and carries no fore-and-aft trysail.

Scale 1:600

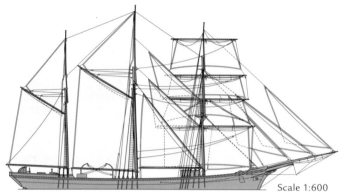

Scale 1:600

Waterwitch of 1871 was launched as a brig but was converted to the barquentine rig after World War I. She has a well-proportioned sail plan and although she has no gaff trysail on the foremast it is interesting to note the boomed main staysail. Also of note is that neither main nor mizzen sail is loosefooted.

and it is quite possible that the barquentine type was considerably more popular in the first half of the century than records imply.

The earliest example of a barquentine seems to have been the experimental ship created by Captain Gower of the East India Company in 1800. Named *Transit* she was designed to be efficient when going to windward, was five-masted and carried three squaresails on the foremast, with fore-and-aft sails on the other four. Most radical were the sprit-like spars that spread the fore-and-aft sails in place of the more typical gaffs and booms. She was built in 1808 and served for a time in the Royal Navy. In 1809 a second, four-masted *Transit* was built, and in 1819 there was a three-masted version.

In 1830 the shipbuilders T & J Brocklebank of Whitehaven, England, launched the three-masted barquentine

(recorded in the yard book as a schooner) *Bonanza*. An elegant, 174-ton vessel, she had well-raked masts and her foremast was so far forward that the course had to be bowsed down to a short bumkin. She was a fast sailer and carried the barquentine rig for eleven years before being converted to a brig. Eight years after *Bonanza*, the three-masted *Loyalist* was launched in Yarmouth, Nova Scotia, but she was converted to barque rig in 1840.

An engraving in the *Illustrated London News*, 1845, shows the American auxiliary steamer *Marmora* with a barquentine rig, and by the 1850s barquentines were being launched on both sides of the Atlantic: the three-masted *Fanny* and *Margaretha* were built in Germany in 1850 and 1851 respectively, *Mary Stockton* was launched in 1853 at Manitowoc on Lake Michigan, and *Kelpie* was built in Aberdeen in 1855 for trade to Gambia – unlike a true barquentine she carried a single yard on her mainmast, presumably to set a squaresail in a fair following wind. Yet still the barquentine remained something of a rarity and it is possible that no more were built in Britain until *Cazique* was launched in Bideford in 1863 and *Eident* was built by James Geddie of Kingston on the Moray Firth the same year. Geddie evidently found some success with the rig, building *Union* (1867), *Zephyr* (1869), *Fiery Cross* (1872), and *Coronella* (1874), all with barquentine sail plans.

Like their close sisters the barques, barquentines became popular in the later days of sail when cost-cutting and crew-reductions became priorities for shipowners. Being predominantly fore-and-aft rigged, unlike barques, they were also well-suited to areas of fickle winds and short-distance trades. It is, perhaps, no coincidence that the last square-rigger to be owned and commercially operated in Britain was a barquentine, *Waterwitch*. Built in 1871 as a brig, she was originally employed in the fruit trade but after World War I was rebuilt and rerigged as a barquentine and employed in the Cornish china clay trade.

Inevitably, the barquentine found greatest popularity in the coast trades and, most particularly, in Baltic and Scandinavian waters where they ranged in size from 300 to 500 tons. In the coastal British type the rigs tended to be baldheaded – the foremast carrying course, double topsails, and a single topgallant, whereas their Scandinavian cousins had loftier rigs and often set a royal on the foremast. Furthermore, the British coasters typically set staysails only from the main- and foremasts whereas the Scandinavians might carry a mizzen-topmast staysail as well as a jib-headed main topsail. (One of the more famous Scandinavian barquentines was the 300-ton 144ft wooden-hulled *Polaris* built by the Framnaes shipyard of Norway – renamed *Endurance* she was Shackleton's vessel on the ill-fated polar expedition of 1914.)

Towards the end of the sailing era, when designers were increasingly experimenting with rigs that would save money, the large steel barquentine briefly found favour. Two typical four-masted examples were *Mozart* and

Beethoven built in 1904 by the Grangemouth and Greenock Dockyard for A.C. de Freitas of Hamburg. Bald-headed and wide on the foremast (*Mozart*'s royal yard was 53ft 6in – as long as some main yards in earlier ships), the three fore-and-aft masts were of equal height (178ft from keel to truck) with fidded topmasts above.

In the late 1800s and early 1900s many ships were converted to barque and barquentine rigs and, especially in North America, additional masts were often fitted to offset the reduced power of fore-and-aft sail compared to square: thus the four-masted ship, *Lord Wolseley* (built by Harland & Wolff, Belfast, in 1883), became a six-masted barquentine in Victoria, British Columbia, in the early 1900s. The *City of Sydney*, built as a barque steamer in Chester, Pennsylvania, in 1875, became a six-masted barquentine in later life. And, in World War I, the US Navy built a number of

Alta, a four-masted barquentine, was built in Glasgow for A P Lorentzen of San Francisco for the timber trade. Her square-rigged foremast was bald-headed with a fidded topgallant mast above a pole lower-and-topmast; all four masts were of equal height. Note the very short gaff on the spanker. (Luke McDonald & Co)

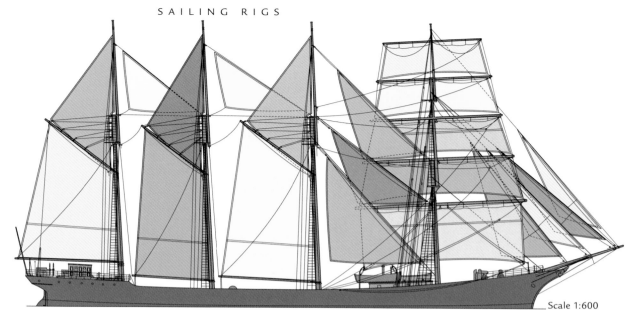

RIGHT AND BELOW RIGHT *Mozart* of 1904 is an example of the barquentine at the height of its development. Built in Scotland for a Hamburg shipping company, her foremast is baldheaded and the sail plan square with double topsails and double topgallants, while her fore-and-aft masts are of equal height but not of equal sail-area – the mizzen trysail is shorter in the foot, the jigger shorter in the luff – leading to a curious mix-and-match appearance.

Scale 1:600

ABOVE *Beethoven* and *Mozart* were built in Scotland in 1904. Bald-headed (no royals) on the foremast, their fore-and-aft masts were of equal height with fidded topmasts. The rig was a compromise between power and economy and was only introduced in the later days of sail. (W A Sherman)

Under almost full sail, this shot of *Aretas* is a fine portrait of a conventional barquentine with foremast carrying course, double topsails, topgallant, royal, and four headsails. The fore-and-aft masts both carry a loose-footed gaff sail and jib-headed topsail.

steamers of which, after the war, seven or eight were converted to six-masted barquentines.

Others of the type ended their days in the Newfoundland fishing trade under Portuguese or French ownership. One such was the *Becca and Mary*, a teak-hulled barquentine built by the Duddon Shipbuilding Company at Millom in Cumbria. Launched in 1904 she was operated by her builder in the home trade for nine years. In 1913 she was sold to Portuguese owners and her name was changed to *Fiueira*, then *Alcion*, and finally *Louzado*. She was rebuilt in the 1940s and increased in size from her original 161.55 tons to 224 tons. She was lost off Newfoundland in 1953.

Never an important rig in the Royal Navy the barquentine was, however, occasionally to be found in service. *Transit*, described earlier, was an early example, and in the late 1880s the navy commissioned nine gunboats of the *Goldfinch* class; all were three-masted barquentines. One of the nine, HMS *Sparrow*, was built by Scott's Shipbuilding and Engineering Company in Greenock in 1889 and served off the coast of Africa before being reposted to Australia in 1900, and finally paid off in 1904. Between 1907 and 1921 she served as a sail-training ship in New Zealand under the name of *Amorkura*. She was broken up in 1955.

Just as the barquentine was never ubiquitous in the era of commercial sail so today its numbers are low in the world's 'heritage' fleets. But there are still some fine examples of later barquentines: *Our Svanen*, built in Frederikssund, Denmark, in 1922 as a three-masted schooner, was rebuilt as a barquentine in Canada for charter and sail-training work. The 247-ton *Marseillois* was built for Mediterranean trade in Valencia, Spain, in 1944, again as a three-masted schooner and is now a floating exhibit, rerigged as a barquentine, in Marseilles, France. And the three-masted *Dewarutji* was built as a barquentine in 1952 in Hamburg, Germany, for the Indonesian Navy for whom she has served as a sail-training vessel ever since.

CHAPTER 4

The Brig

The brig *Marie Sophie* was built as *Marie* in 1879 and is representative of the peak of development in European brigs. Her masts are tall and both are in three sections; she sets a course, double topsails, single topgallant, and royal on each. Her gaff-rigged spanker is loose-footed and she has no fore trysail (a sail more popular on American brigs – relatively fewer in number – than British). An attractive vessel, she remained in service until being lost in 1902.

Possibly the most successful of all square rigs, the brig served in naval and commercial arenas on both sides of the Atlantic. From the mid 1700s to the late 1800s it was the most popular all-purpose rig.

DEFINITION

The brig has two masts, square rigged on both. The sails and masts – in name and construction – are as found on the full-rigged ship (see p.8). A variant of the brig (and often confused with it, both in the past and today) is the snow. This rig is also two-masted and also fully square on both masts; however, it has an additional trysail mast abaft the mainmast and the luff of the gaff spanker is laced or hooped to this. Thus, the snow can carry a main course that will not be fouled by the spanker. Although not a prerequisite of the type, the snow's spanker is often

loose-footed and large compared to that of the brig. In both the snow and the brig the standing gaff is common and it is rare to see the trysail furled down to the boom. (The term 'snow' seems to have been lost in American usage in the late 1790s although after 1800 most US Navy two-masted men-of-war were snows rather than brigs.)

Further variations include the jackass brig, a term much used among American sailors to describe a brig with no square main course and a two-piece foremast. The term was also used to describe the 'brigantines' used in Newfoundland and Labrador from 1850, which could alter their mainmast to carry squaresails in the summer but sent the yards down in the winter to convert to fore-and-aft sails. The hermaphrodite brig was fully square on the foremast and fore-and-aft on the main (see brigantine p.44). Finally, the polacca brig, seen in north Devon and the Bristol Channel in the mid 1800s, and in Germany as late as the 1880s, had two masts setting squaresails, but they were in single poles rather than the usual three pieces. In France polacca brigs sometimes had a single-pole foremast and a two-piece main. English polaccas typically carried a square foresail, topsail, and topgallant, a gaff mainsail, and either square or jib-headed main topsails. The topsail and topgallant yards were lowered to the course for furling. Some Continental European polaccas of the 1860s carried courses, topsails, and topgallants on both masts and lowered the topsail but not the topgallant yards.

HISTORY

The brig was much favoured as a naval vessel. Although it had its origins in the small vessels of the seventeenth and even sixteenth centuries, it emerged in the early eighteenth

Scale 1:500

Found on both naval and merchant vessels the brig was a long-lived and popular rig. Here the development is seen from the European snow of the mid 1700s to the American naval brig of the mid 1800s.

1 The snow's spanker is set on a separate mast abaft the mainmast, thus allowing the setting of an unimpeded main course.

2 *Newton*, built in England in 1788, is interesting for her pole (one-piece) foremast and well-raked mainmast.

3 A typical British collier brig of 1800 carries a workmanlike rig without main course but with a yard for a spritsail.

4 The Royal Navy *Cruizer* class of 1796 – the most numerous class of warship built in the age of sail – has a relatively tall rig with deep topsails and studding sails on the foremast.

5 The German brig, *Leopard*, of 1803, has a similar rig to the *Cruizer*, although without studding sails, but with a fore gaff trysail and longer bowsprit.

6 Built for speed the American slaving brig, *Dos Amigos* of 1822, has very deep courses and well-raked masts.

7 *Ouragan*, a French slaver of 1830, carries a squarer rig designed for speed but probably less efficient to windward.

8 A typical Royal Navy brig of 1840 – the rig is suprisingly similar to that of the *Cruizer* of 1802.

9 *August von Wismar*, a German merchant brig of 1840, has a similar though smaller rig to *Leopard* and would have had a smaller crew – unlike the Royal Navy brig of the same era.

10 The American naval brig *Somers* of 1844 carries a spencer (gaff-rigged trysail) on her foremast and has well-raked masts, reminiscent of the American schooners.

1   2   3   4

5   6   7

8   9   10

century (as a snow) and then again in the late 1700s when it was a true brig. (Confusingly, Royal Navy brigs were known as brigs when under the command of a Lieutenant, but brig-sloops under a Commander.)

The naval brig was highly versatile and the rig was suited to vessels of up to 20 guns, as well as smaller vessels employed in reconnaissance, escort duties, and coastal patrol. Not only were they heavily armed for their size, they were also fast and seaworthy and proved themselves so invaluable that by 1806 the brig-sloop had become the largest single type in the Royal Navy. At that time two new brig classes were built in considerable number. The *Cruizer* had a very high rig setting skysails above the royals and a long-boomed spanker. Facing several defeats in the American War of 1812, the *Cruizer* class fell out of favour, but not before more than one hundred had been built to the design. The smaller 10-gun *Cherokee* was fast but, perhaps, over-rigged – vessels of the *Cherokee* class gained the nickname 'coffin brigs' as they had a reputation for being wrecked. (Curiously HMS *Beagle* – made famous as a survey vessel under the command of Robert Fitzroy with Charles Darwin in the company – was built as a *Cherokee* in 1823 but was refitted as a barque for her survey work.)

In the late 1700s Royal Navy gunboats were also re-rigged as brigs and employed firstly as defensive vessels in British coastal waters; then off the French and Dutch coasts, again in defensive roles; and finally, by the turn of

the century, were sent anywhere the Navy thought they might be made useful.

Thus, in the 1800s the brig became the most popular naval cruiser throughout Europe; and even in America, where the schooner was more favoured, it made its mark. Five brigs were built in the United States in the 1840s: the *Somers*, the *Bainbridge*, the *Truxton*, the *Perry*, and the *Lawrence*. The last was relatively deep-draughted and of limited use, but the other four were very fast and highly

LEFT *Phoenix* was built as a schooner in 1929, was converted to a brigantine in 1974, to a caravel in 1991, and at last to a brig with single topsails and topgallants in 1996. (Dalgleish Images Ltd)

RIGHT 'A Brig off the Coast' by J. Murday, 1888. On a merchant brig with false, painted gunports, the crew is reducing sail: the royals are already furled, the main topgallant sheets have been let fly, and the fore topgallant is being furled by two crewmen. Under her stern can be seen a brigantine while under her bow are a small lugger raising reduced dipping foresail, the mainmast having been lowered, and another brig sailing away with no sails set above the topsails. (Royal Exchange Art Gallery, London)

regarded. The 105ft *Perry*, launched in 1843, was considered the US Navy's fastest sailing ship and gained fame in 1850 when she captured the *Martha*, the largest slaving ship ever known.

Because of their speed brigs were much employed by the United States and Royal Navies to combat the illegal pursuits of piracy and slavery. Two of the most successful in this role were *Waterwitch*, designed as a yacht and purchased by the Royal Navy as a slave-cruiser, and *Black Joke*,

originally a Baltimore-built slave-brig, the *Henriquetta*, captured by the British in 1820.

From the middle 1700s the brig and snow were the rigs of choice in Britain for small- and medium-sized merchant vessels. They required smaller crews than the three-masted barques and full-rigged ships, were powerful, seaworthy, and manoeuvrable in restricted waters. Of all brigs the most important was undoubtedly the collier brig of the East Coast of England. Hundreds were built to sail between the

A brig sailing in the Black Sea, her well-patched sails evidence of long use; she was probably one of the last sailing traders, although the date of the picture is unknown. (James Randell)

coalfields of the northeast and the Pool of London delivering fuel to the southeast's industrial heartland and the densely populated capital city. Designed as bulk carriers with shallow draught they were typically bluff-bowed and had flat sterns but were highly manoeuvrable and capable of sailing up the Thames as it wound its way from estuary to city. In their prime they had single topsails although later examples had doubles. The fore course tended to be narrow and set to a bentinck boom (*ie* a spar used to stretch the foot of the sail) so that the sail could be controlled with a single sheet to the boom and light guys on either side; thus the fore course could still be carried in confined stretches – such as river and estuary waters – and handled by a relatively small crew even when the vessel was having to repeatedly alter course. The collier brigs carried comparatively tall rigs capable of pushing their heavily laden hulls through the short seas and strong currents of the North Sea and Thames estuary. In later years, when the hulls were somewhat more refined, some collier brigs traded to mainland Europe in the summer months when the hometrade was less profitable.

In the first half of the nineteenth century brigs were to be found in almost all trades. In Britain they were employed in the coastal trades between homeports and to the Continent. And, although they would be later replaced by the topsail schooner, they were also used in the West Indian and fruit trades. The brig was also the favoured vessel for the Hooghly River pilots in India.

Wherever their homeport and whatever their influences, brigs around the world shared the essentials of the rig although sail plans varied according to size of hull – larger vessels set royals, while smaller examples carried nothing above the topgallants (later British brigs of all sizes typically set no royal on the foremast and often no royals at all). Some carried gaff trysails on spencer masts abaft the foremast (as well as the fore course) although this was more common in American than British brigs. For the most part brigs of the 1800s were small – between 100 and 200 tons – and many of less than 100 tons were built in the first

decades of the century; a few were even of less than 50 tons. Few were built of iron. However, a Royal Navy brig of 1875 bucked the trend of both material and size: the iron-hulled *Temeraire* was of 8,540 tons and had the longest lower masts and yards ever made for the British fleet; her load waterline length was 280ft, her beam 60ft. She was paid off in 1891 and broken up in 1921.

In America brigs became very popular towards the end of the eighteenth century in the West Indian trade, and during the Revolutionary War many fast examples were built (and again in the War of 1812) for blockade running and privateering. After the wars several such brigs went into slave trading.

By the mid 1800s the brig was at last being overtaken by other more economically efficient rigs: in the south and southwest of England it was the schooner, while elsewhere in British waters, as speed became less important and capacity of greater, the barque became more popular. Of those brigs built in Britain in the later 1800s many were quickly converted to brigantine, barque, or barquentine. In America the favourites were the hermaphrodite brig, and brigantine and ubiquitous schooner.

The last brigs to remain in the merchant trades were in the Baltic and Mediterranean, but surprisingly few have survived, even in the world's heritage fleets. However, the brig is a popular rig for sail training and several vessels were so built in the late twentieth century: *Lady Washington*, 112ft and 99 tons, was built at Grays Harbor Historical Seaport in Aberdeen, Washington, in 1989 as a reproduction of the original vessel of the same name – the first American vessel to visit the West Coast. Another reconstruction, *Niagara*, was built in 1988, a copy of the warship taken into victory against the British by Oliver Hazard Perry at the Battle of Lake Erie in 1813. And in Britain the first brig to be launched in the twentieth century was the steel-hulled 95ft TS *Royalist* built by Groves and Guttridge of Cowes, Isle of Wight, in 1971. One of the few snows still sailing is *Pilgrim* built in Denmark in 1945 as a replica of the vessel immortalized by Richard Henry Dana in his book *Two Years Before the Mast*.

The Brigantine

The term 'brigantine' has led to considerable confusion amongst sailing-rig definitions. The 'true brigantine' was a rig of the early eighteenth century but it was in the nineteenth century that the 'modern brigantine' emerged as a type, which, in combining square and fore-and-aft sails, answered an economic need just as the larger barquentine did. One of the most famous vessels of all time, the *Mary Celeste*, was a brigantine launched in Nova Scotia in 1861.

DEFINITION

The true brigantine of the early 1700s was a two-masted vessel, fully square on the fore, and fore-and-aft on the main, with square main topsails. It was different from the brig only in the construction of the mainmast which was in two pieces – lower and top – rather than three. The modern brigantine (also known as the 'hermaphrodite brig' – most commonly in America – a 'brig-schooner' in Britain, and a 'half-brig' in New England) is fully square on the foremast and fore-and-aft with no yards on the main. In the nineteenth century the mainmast typically had a single set of crosstrees that could be as wide as the ship's beam so that the topmast had no standing rigging other than backstays and a single shroud running out to either end of the crosstrees. The last commercial brigantines ranged in size from about 100 to 300 tons.

A less common variant was the polacca brigantine, which could be as small as 10 tons and as large as 300 tons. Here, one or both masts were in a single piece from keel to truck and, apart from backstays, had no standing rigging above the lower shrouds. The foremast had a course, double topsails, and a topgallant, and gear was reduced to a minimum throughout.

HISTORY

Brigantines were recorded as far back as the late 1600s. In his book, *History of American Sailing Ships*, Howard I Chapelle wrote that the term 'brigantine' appeared in pre-1700 colonial records and that the type was second in number only to the sloop – although the classification probably referred to brigs, snows, and brigantines.

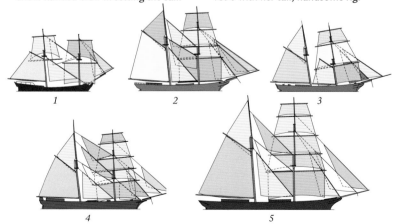

1 Strictly speaking the only 'true' brigantine illustrated here, this anonymous vessel of the early eighteenth century differs from the brig of the previous chapter in having a fore-and-aft mainmast *but with* a square topsail.
2 *Caroline* of 1863 was a typical 'brigantine' (or hermaphrodite brig) of the mid nineteenth century – note the 'Bentinck' boom at the foot of the fore course, which would have helped a short-handed crew in setting the sail.

3 Of similar era *Regulus*, 1867, has no Bentinck, carries a deep single topsail, and a spencer on the foremast.
4 A typical trading brigantine of the late nineteenth century *Raven* was launched at Prince Edward Island in 1875. She has double topsails, topgallant, and royal above the fore course, and a full gaff mainsail.
5 By the end of the nineteenth century the brigantine had fully evolved as can be seen in this German example of 1890 with her tall, handsome rig.

1   *2*   *3*

4   *5*

The brigantine *Courtney Ford* (possibly of San Francisco) sailing with a large deck cargo. Her foremast sails are conventional – course, double topsails, topgallant, royal, and skysail – but the sails on her mainmast are curious: they have the appearance of a cut-down or jury rig where once she would surely have had a gaff spanker and jib-headed topsail.

Nevertheless, it is indisputable that the brigantine (as we know it, the 'true' brigantine) did indeed exist at this early date, as there is contemporary iconographic evidence.

By the mid 1720s the type had been firmly established: a vessel with two masts, square-rigged on the fore and fore-and-aft on the main, with or without a square topsail, was a brigantine. However, at some time in the middle of the century, a further complication set in: the term 'brigantine' was abbreviated to 'brig'. In the first edition of his *Universal Dictionary of the Marine*, published in 1769, Falconer makes an entry for 'Brig or Brigantine'. Thus, through the 1700s, the three rigs: brig, snow, and brigantine, co-existed and were, to an extent, interchangeable by definition.

Leon, an example of a typical coastal trading brigantine with double topsails, topgallant, and royal, here sailing under the Norwegian flag. (Adamson, Rothesay)

were both officially classified as 'square-rigged' the two-masted brigantine was not; masters holding no more than a fore-and-aft certificate could, and did, take command of a brigantine, but not of a brig or barquentine.

In America the brigantine held on for a time in the West Indies and transatlantic trades but was, inevitably, superseded by the less labour-intensive three-masted schooner. Nevertheless, in North America brigantines were still being built around the turn of the century: *Galilee* was built at Benicia, California, in 1891 as a brigantine with topgallant and royal on her foremast. She was a fast vessel and, on her maiden voyage, set a new record from San Francisco to Tahiti of nineteen days. In 1907–08 she was chartered to research compass variation in the Pacific, and in about 1912 was sold into the fish trade and rerigged as a three-masted baldheaded schooner. As late as 1910 new brigantines – like the 125ft *Viola* launched in Provincetown, Massachusetts – were being built on the east coast of America and Canada for whaling.

However, as the 1800s came to a close few new brigantines were being built in Britain and those that did remain in trade were often old and tired and making do with

Even in the 1800s, as the snow and brig began to merge, and the modern brigantine became a definite type, the records show a curious reluctance to use the classification. The shipbuilder Alexander Hall of Aberdeen, Scotland, built a brigantine, *Matilda,* in 1829; she was described as a 'square-sterned schooner or hermaphrodite'.

Like almost all developments in commercial sail, the evolution of the modern brigantine was determined by economics – primarily the rising cost of manpower and maintenance. The earlier 'true' brigantine was, effectively, a brig in all but her lack of main topgallant mast and, while she was as expensive to run as the fully square brig, she lacked that type's sailing performance. In short, she lost out on both counts. It made sense, therefore, to remove the main yards and raise a jib-headed main topsail in their place.

Brigantines were built for commercial fleets on both sides of the Atlantic, but never in great numbers. In Britain, however, they did continue in service into the twentieth century thanks to a loophole in British Merchant Shipping law: while the three-masted barquentine and two-masted brig

Built in 1938 as a non-magnetic survey vessel for the British government, *Research* was, at 142ft 6in, possibly the largest purpose-built brigantine. Her rig is typical of the trading brigantines that preceded her towards the end of the nineteenth century and would have been handy and efficient. However, *Research* was a victim of World War II: only partially fitted out by September 1939, she was laid up and finally broken up due to a lack of funding.

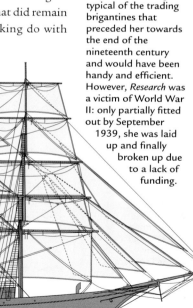

Scale 1:600

The brigantine *Polly* was tender to BTS *Formidable* in Portishead, near Bristol. Her rig is conventional with course, single topsail, topgallants and royal on the foremast, loose-footed gaff and jib-headed topsail on the main together with multiple staysails on both masts.

reduced sail areas and cast-off gear from other vessels.

Prior to the brigantine's latterday rise in popularity amongst sail-training aficionados, possibly the last to be built for commercial purposes were *Research* in Dartmouth, England, and *Soren Larsen*, in Denmark. The former was commissioned by the Admiralty for magnetic, atmospheric, and oceanographic survey. She was completed in 1939 but was immediately laid up for the duration of the war. She never sailed and was broken up in 1952. Conversely, the wooden-hulled *Soren Larsen* was launched in 1949 by Soren

Larsen & Sons and traded throughout the Baltic as well as to British and other European ports carrying general cargo, timber, and grain until 1972. She was restored in Colchester, England, in the late 1970s and today works in sail training around the world. In the latter half of the twentieth century the brigantine has proved a favourite in training fleets and several new brigantines have been launched, particularly in North America. The most recent were the *Exy Johnson* and the *Irving Johnson*, two 90ft brigantines built by the Los Angeles Maritime Institute.

CHAPTER 6

The Sloop

Built between 1987 and 1992 by students of WoodenBoat School, Brooklin, Maine, to reworked lines from 1907, the Friendship sloop, *Belford Gray*, is typical of her type. Her multiple headsails – she can set a flying jib as sell as the staysail and jib seen here – may lead to confusion between the classifications 'cutter' and 'sloop', but her fixed bowsprit and stayed jib define her as a sloop. Note, too, that her mast is considerably further forward than would be the case on a cutter. (Benjamin Mendlowitz)

The seemingly simple 'sloop' is another area for confusion in rig classification and has gone through many definitions relating to hull shape, details of rig, principal use, and more. But the term was eventually accepted as a specific rig type from the middle of the nineteenth century.

DEFINITION

Depending on place and time 'sloop' has meant different things to different people. In the Netherlands of the sixteenth century the 'sloep' was a ship's open rowing boat. In seventeenth-century Britain a sloop might be an open oared or sailed boat used for transporting goods or people to and from a ship. In the Royal Navy of the seventeenth, eighteenth, and nineteenth centuries a sloop of war was a small vessel that carried guns on its upper deck; its rig might be full, brig, or ketch (see pp.8, 38, 60), and furthermore, depending on the rank of its commanding officer, it would be classified a ship-sloop (captain) or a brig-sloop (commander). Before the mid 1800s in Britain a gaff-rigged coastal trader with two headsails might be a sloop; it differed from a 'cutter' (see p.54) in having a fixed bowsprit, a stayed jib, and a beamy, relatively shallow-draught hull designed for load-carrying rather than speed.

By the mid nineteenth century, however, the modern definition had been established: a single-masted, fore-and-aft-rigged vessel carrying a single headsail set to a forestay. Some sloops, most commonly working boats or those deriving from working-boat types, set a temporary headsail in light airs giving rise to confusion with the modern definition of a cutter. A further, albeit loose, defining of the term is that the mainsail tends to be larger than that of a cutter and the mast is typically stepped further

forward. Today the sloop is the most common of all sailing rigs and can be used on any vessel from a traditional small working boat to the most high-tech ocean-going racer.

HISTORY

As a rig type the sloop began in the Netherlands. Originally a late-sixteenth-century term for a ship's rowing boat the 'sloep' grew in size into the next century and gained a single-mast rig. As the type became more efficient so it quickly spread into many trades throughout the Low Countries until it was to be found on a vast number of commercial boats of varying sizes and types. The earliest examples had a tall mast stepped well forward, which carried a sprit-rigged mainsail and an overlapping staysail. Later the most common rig combined a gaff mainsail – with a short, usually hooked, gaff – and single headsail hanked to a forestay; sometimes, as in the case of the Dutch boeiers and botters of the eighteenth and nineteenth centuries a jib would be set flying to the end of the bowsprit in light airs.

The rig was also found around the shores of the Baltic Sea and on the fjords of Norway where the smallest open boats such as faerings, bindalsbåts, and hardangerbåts, that once set a single squaresail (see p.10), evolved to a small fore-and-aft rig of sprit mainsail and forestaysail tacked inboard to the stem.

By the middle of the 1700s the type had spread across the North Sea and into Britain, where the sprit rig was quickly replaced by the gaff. The rig was adopted by various indigenous commercial workboats such as the Humber keel – a bluff-bowed barge of about 60ft in length that was traditionally square-rigged on a single mast. In the late

In modern times one of the simplest of rigs, the sloop has had a long and varied history.

1 A Royal Navy longboat of the early to mid 1700s was essentially a sloop with a running bowsprit for a jib.

2 A British colonial sloop as used in Bermuda in the mid 1700s, with gaff spanker, extremely deep course, double topsails, and jib-boom.

3 The mid-eighteenth-century Dutch boeier – with gaff mainsail and single headsail – could rig a bowsprit with jib for a 'summer' rig.

4 *Clio*, an early merchant sloop built in England in 1816, with both fore-and-aft and square sails. Her similarity to the Leith smack (see drawing [2] p.55)

exemplifies the confusion between sloop and cutter definitions. Her bowsprit is fixed, her jib stayed.

5 *Maria*, a privately-owned yacht of 1845, was an out-and-out racing sloop.

6 A New England sailing dory of the late 1870s – a low and simple rig for a simple boat.

7 Of a similar era, the North Carolina seine boat carries a taller sprit-rigged mainsail with the added sophistication of a jib-headed topsail.

8 A true Bermudian sloop at the peak of the type's development in the late 1880s – note the low sprit in place of a boom.

9 Although similar to the rig of many

small boats of the Mediterranean, in America the lateen rig plus jib was unique to the feluccas of San Francisco and were to be seen in numbers in the last two decades of the 1800s.

10 The skipjack of Chesapeake Bay carries a rig remarkably similar to that of the late Bermudian sloop (8), but each sail is boomed.

11 The elegant Hudson River sloop of the late nineteenth century set a simple but powerful gaff-rigged mainsail with jib-headed topsail.

12 The workmanlike rig of the early twentieth-century Humber sloop often had a high-peaked mainsail without topsail and (as seen here) a boomed staysail.

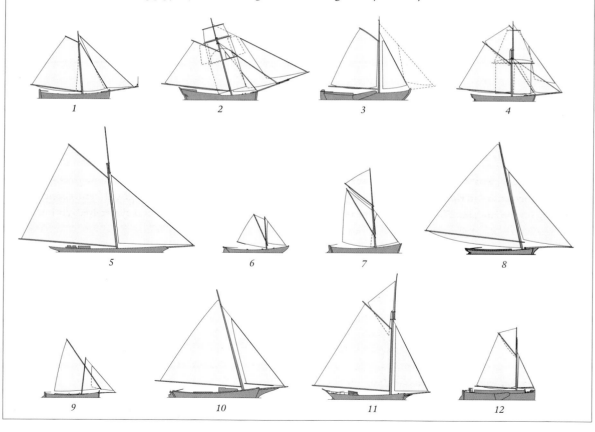

1

2

3

4

5

6

7

8

9

10

11

12

1800s the type developed into more refined vessels with a fore-and-aft rig – despite having two headsails (a staysail and a jib) the type was known as the Humber sloop; a few were still working as coal carriers in the late 1930s. Similar to the Humber sloop the billy boy of the early 1800s was also sloop rigged until rising labour costs forced a need to reduce crew sizes and the large mainsail was replaced by the split rig of the ketch (see p.60). In the west of England on many inland rivers, sloops of varying kinds were used for cargo work: salt went from Droitwich to Gloucester on sloop-rigged trows; coal went from Liverpool to Winsford on sprit-rigged sloops known as flats; in Somerset small (16–23ft) open boats called flatners carried peat to market, whithies to basket makers, and perhaps even sheep from South Wales to Bridgwater.

The early sloops of colonial America almost certainly arrived with the Dutch. As they became a defined group they included small vessels of 25–70 tons with a gaff mainsail and two or three headsails, square topsail, and sometimes a course. They were engaged in coastal trade, whaling, fishing, or privateering, and during the American Revolution sailed as armed sloops of war.

Among the most famous of all American sloops were the Hudson River sloops of New York, which worked the river from the middle of the seventeenth century until the latter half of the nineteenth – in the 1790s there were as many as 100 trading on the Hudson. The rig had become recognisable by the early 1700s: a tall mast stepped well forward and with a pronounced rake. The short-gaffed mainsail had a long boom that overhung the stern, while the large jib was tacked to a short, heavy, steeved-up bowsprit. As the century progressed the mast became straighter and the gaff longer. Although the type was still being built in the 1870s it was fast being replaced by the schooner (see p.73).

The sloop rig found favour right across America, from the Caribbean to the Great Lakes, from New England to California. For the most part, it was used on open boats working inshore. There were small sailing-and-rowing boats: the sailing dories, the Seabright skiff of New Jersey,

the Noank sloop (popular from Long Island to Cape Cod), the seine boats of North Carolina, to name but a few; they carried a main spritsail and overlapping headsail (the North Carolina boats were unique in carrying a jib-headed topsail that could be raised and lowered independent of the mainsail). On San Francisco Bay there were the feluccas that set a single lateen sail (see p.89) on a forward-raking mast with a jib set flying to a bowsprit.

Larger boats included the lobster boats of New England, latterly known as Friendship sloops. These ranged in size from 16ft to 40ft on deck. The smaller models set a gaff mainsail and a staysail but in later years larger boats often had a staysail, jib, gaff topsail, and jib topsail. In all the mast was stepped far forward. The Quoddy boats of the Canadian Maritime Provinces and Downeast Maine ranged from 20ft to 40ft and, in the larger boats, had a gaff mainsail and a jib set to a standing bowsprit; the smaller versions had a running bowsprit that would be set with a flying jib in summer; in winter these boats carried only the mainsail. The Texas scow had a simple rig of gaff mainsail and jib on a slightly forward-raking mast. The skipjacks of Chesapeake Bay set jib-headed mainsails and club-footed jibs on well-raked masts stepped in hulls that could be as long as 60ft on deck. But perhaps the most spectacular of all were the sandbaggers of New York. Developed through the 1800s these shallow-draughted centreboard boats began as general workboats and oyster dredgers but ended as radically over-canvassed racers with huge overhanging gaff mainsails and large boomed jibs set to long bowsed-down bowsprits.

The islanders of Bermuda and the Bahamas have long been famous for their sloop-rigged boats. The type evolved from small working boats used for inter-island transport and fishing. The early rig consisted of short-gaff mainsails with low horizontal sprits rather than booms, and single overlapping jibs set on short bowsprits. By the mid 1800s in Bermuda the mainsail had become universally jib-headed, and by the end of the century the mast had a distinct rake and both the sprit and bowsprit had extended dramatically to allow for a large spread of sail. In Bermuda the type gradually died out, the last being built in 1899, but the Bahama version – a short-gaff mainsail with a mast nearly twice as high as the boat is long and a mainsprit that greatly overhangs the stern – is still raced in annual regattas.

The sloop rig made it into yachting as early as the 1850s (although many of the earliest examples were later converted to schooners and cutters), but was particularly favoured from the turn of the century. In the 1920s the jib-headed mainsail gained popularity with one-design and other racing classes large and small, and the sloop finally emerged in its modern-day configuration of narrow mainsail with ¾- or masthead-rigged staysail. The gaff sloop did hang on but became increasingly rare in new-builds – latterly it has made a minor comeback in 'retro-classic' designs. As rigging and sail-cloth technologies have developed through the twentieth and into the twenty-first centuries, the 'bermudan sloop' rig has become the most common standard for racing and cruising yachts and dinghies, with the current trend favouring small mainsails and large overlapping staysails known as genoas, and for downwind sailing, unstayed balloon sails – spinnakers.

Scale 1:100

ABOVE The beach boats of Aberdaron, Wales, were built for lobster and herring fishing from the mid 1800s. All under 15ft in length and with high-peaked gaff mainsail and small jib tacked on to a short iron bowsprit, their rig was simple but effective; the boats could be handled easily by two men. Although the fishery in which they worked has long since collapsed, thirty of the boats survive and are raced through the summer as a restricted class.

BELOW Perhaps the most extreme of all sloops, the sandbaggers started out as general workboats in New York Harbor but evolved through the 1800s to become over-canvassed ultimate racing machines. A 27ft boat might have a 40ft boom and a bowsprit extending 23ft beyond the stem; the overall length (from jib tack to mainsail clew) could thus reach 68ft – more than double the length of the hull!

RIGHT Today's most common yacht rig, the 'bermudan' sloop – a narrow jib-headed mainsail with masathead-rigged staysail – in this instance a large overlapping genoa jib. (Dalgleish Images Ltd)

Scale 1:200

B&Q circumnavigated the world in record time in 2005. Although she has multiple headsails on multiple forestays, she sets only one at a time and, according to her designer Nigel Irens, can be defined as a 'bermudan sloop'. As pictured she is sailing fast under reefed main and smallest jib. (Benoit Stichelbaut/ DPPI/Offshore Challenges)

The Cutter

In its first use the term 'cutter' referred to a hull type but, while the world's navies still use the term for specific craft – with or without sailing rigs – it has been used to describe a single-masted rig since the late eighteenth century.

DEFINITION

There is evidence of the word 'cutter' from at least the middle of the eighteenth century and, for the most part, it referred to a fast sailing vessel usually, but not always, with a single mast. However, the Royal Navy also used the term for its ship's boats; these were anything from 16ft to 34ft in length and were known as cutters even though they were typically rigged as lugsail ketches (the Royal Navy still has 'cutters' – small boats with a mainsail and jib and either four or eight

oars). Beyond the navy, in Britain the word initially referred to a hull type – beamy, fast, sharp-bowed – and the term 'cutter-built' could apply to any such vessel, be it cutter, schooner, or brig. However, as the eighteenth century progressed, 'cutter' was increasingly used to describe a particular rig: a single, usually aft-raked, mast stepped about one-third or two-fifths of the water-line length back from the bow, a gaff mainsail (often loose-footed), a topsail, and two or more headsails – the jib set flying to a running bowsprit. One or more squaresails could be carried, although these became less common in the nineteenth century. The sail area was often vast in relation to the size of hull and the type was almost always associated with speed.

The 'cutter' and the 'sloop' have often been confused and,

This example of a Royal Navy cutter of the mid 1700s has an extraordinary array of sails. Principal are the gaff mainsail, main course, topsail, topgallant, and staysail. Light-weather sails are the jib and flying jib set on the long running bowsprit, upper and lower topsail studding sails, a watersail beneath the main boom and a ring-tail outboard of the mainsail's leech. The many reef points testify to the expectation that such a cutter would sail in all weathers.

While considerably more conservative, and at first glance vastly different, when seen alongside the Royal Navy cutter, the rig of *Jolie Brise*, a French pilot cutter built in 1913, has obvious links to her predecessor of 150 years. Really, all that has gone are the squaresails. The main gaff-rigged sail now has a large jib-headed topsail and the three headsails – staysail, jib and flying jib on a running (albeit shorter) bowsprit – are still there.

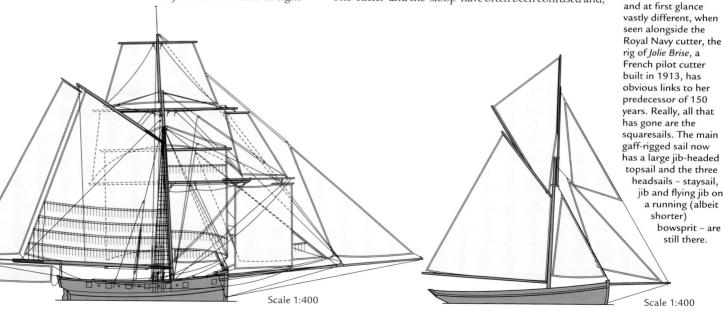

Scale 1:400

Scale 1:400

indeed, there remains a difference in definition between American and British classifications. The most important facet of the early definition was that the bowsprit of a cutter was running – *ie* it could be brought into the vessel in heavy weather or in port, or extended to its full length for increased sail carrying – whereas the sloop's bowsprit was fixed. In Britain 'cutter' has latterly come to mean any single-masted vessel with more than one headsail. However, in America such a vessel could be a 'sloop' for here the placement of the mast and the set-up of the bowsprit are all important – thus a Friendship sloop (see p.48) might in Britain be described as 'cutter rigged' on account of its headsails, but in America is a 'sloop' because of its forward-stepped mast and its forestay that runs to the end of the fixed bowsprit rather than the stemhead.

Today the cutter rig, as used in leisure craft, is single-masted with a gaff or jib-headed mainsail, and two or more headsails, with or without a bowsprit, fixed or running. The mast is still typically stepped well back from the stem.

HISTORY

The history of the cutter rig is essentially British. Designed for speed, its links with fast sailing were so strong that in 1784, in an attempt to curb smuggling activities, the British Government passed an act stating that no privately-owned vessel could be cutter-rigged (*ie* have a running bowsprit with flying jib). Being almost impossible to enforce the legislation had little effect. At about that time cutters were developing in British waters to be the extreme vessels of the day: lightly built, they set vast sail areas and were employed in any activity where speed, rather than capacity, was of the essence. The naval cutter had a well-raked mast on which was set a large loose-footed gaff mainsail (in light airs the mainsail was extended beyond the leech by an additional vertical sail – a ringtail – and below the boom by a small horizontal sail – a watersail), a course, topsail, topgallant, and sometimes royal (all or some of which could be extended with studdingsails), a forestay-sail, jib, and flying jib. The rig was typically set on a relatively

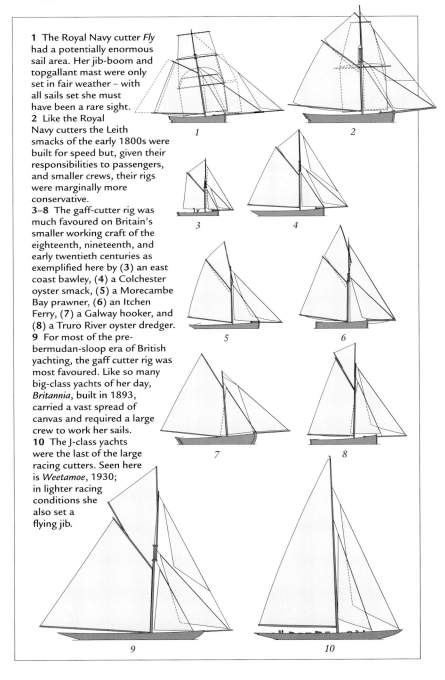

1 The Royal Navy cutter *Fly* had a potentially enormous sail area. Her jib-boom and topgallant mast were only set in fair weather – with all sails set she must have been a rare sight.
2 Like the Royal Navy cutters the Leith smacks of the early 1800s were built for speed but, given their responsibilities to passengers, and smaller crews, their rigs were marginally more conservative.
3–8 The gaff-cutter rig was much favoured on Britain's smaller working craft of the eighteenth, nineteenth, and early twentieth centuries as exemplified here by (**3**) an east coast bawley, (**4**) a Colchester oyster smack, (**5**) a Morecambe Bay prawner, (**6**) an Itchen Ferry, (**7**) a Galway hooker, and (**8**) a Truro River oyster dredger.
9 For most of the pre-bermudan-sloop era of British yachting, the gaff cutter rig was most favoured. Like so many big-class yachts of her day, *Britannia*, built in 1893, carried a vast spread of canvas and required a large crew to work her sails.
10 The J-class yachts were the last of the large racing cutters. Seen here is *Weetamoe*, 1930; in lighter racing conditions she also set a flying jib.

1

2

3

4

5

6

7

8

9

10

small hull (the running bowsprit could often be longer than the deck) and was manned by a large, highly experienced crew. Such vessels were used by the Royal Navy as cruisers, 'advice' boats, or for chasing privateers, and also by the Revenue Office for intercepting smugglers, by Trinity House (responsible for lighthouses around the coasts of England, Wales, and the Channel Isles) as lighthouse tenders, by the Post Office as packet boats, and, of course, by the smugglers and privateers themselves.

Less extreme examples of the rig were used on fishing boats and in passenger service. Typical of the latter were the Leith smacks which, throughout the 1800s, carried people between London and Edinburgh. Fuller than the naval cutters and with less dramatic sail plans, the smacks were, nevertheless, also designed for speed – in the early days simply to save their landlubber passengers from being at sea for any longer than necessary, and in the later 1800s, because they had to compete with the ever-improving road and rail networks. There is claim of a Leith smack sailing the 460 miles from London to Edinburgh in 42 hours, but typically

LEFT The Truro River oyster dredger, one of the last commercial fishing boats still working under sail in the West. The versatility of the cutter rig is here evidenced on a windy day – despite setting only a well-reefed mainsail, staysail, and spitfire jib, the boat is still balanced and sailing well. (Jenny Bennett)

RIGHT 'Entrance to a River' by Thomas Luny, 1806. Two cutters beat out from the shore in rough weather. Both appear to have reefed their mainsails and neither has set a topsail although they certainly would have carried one for lighter airs. (Royal Exchange Art Gallery, London)

Ireland (where the indigenous 'hookers' were used for coastal trade and transportation as well as for fishing), and Scandinavia. Today, on the Fal and Truro Rivers in Cornwall cutter-rigged workboats are still used for dredging oysters in the winter months – the last commercially viable sail-and-oar fishery in the Western World.

For cargo-carrying the cutter was soon surpassed in Northern Europe by the schooner and ketch but in some British waters the rig continued in local coastal trade throughout the nineteenth century. In the West Country the cutters, or trading smacks, were much used around the coasts of Devon, Cornwall, and Somerset. Smaller, shallower-draught barges (sometimes confusingly called 'sloops') were also used in Plymouth and Falmouth; while on the River Severn cutter-rigged trows with very shoal draught and poor windward performance were used for carrying local cargoes.

Today, perhaps the most famous of all Britain's working cutters are the Bristol Channel pilot cutters, of which several have survived, converted for pleasure sailing. In its heyday in the late nineteenth century the type averaged about 40ft–50ft on deck and carried a cutter rig with the mast set well back from the stem, giving a fair-sized gaff mainsail, a jib-headed topsail (on either a topmast or pole mast; where a topmast was carried it was often sent down in winter), a large staysail, and a jib. Jibs of several sizes were carried and set according to the weather: there was a working jib for easy conditions, a 'spitfire' for heavy weather, and a 'spinnaker' jib, whose luff reached from bowsprit end to masthead, for light airs. The cutters were typically manned by a crew of three – the pilot and two others, one of whom would usually be a 'boy'. Pilots from other coasts also used cutter-rigged boats. In Devon and Cornwall they were often larger – in the Isles of Scilly several were over 65ft long – while in northern France they were similar to those of the Bristol Channel, although many say they were faster and more able. *Jolie Brise*, built as a pilot boat for Le Havre, France, in 1913, was converted to a yacht and won many races – among them the Bermuda

The 34-ton Falmouth pilot cutter *Vincent* in Falmouth Bay, Cornwall. Obviously in no hurry, the mainsail has been reefed. The flag atop her mast indicates the presence of a pilot on board. *Vincent* was built in Stonehouse, Plymouth, in 1852.

the fastest smacks sailed the distance in 50–54 hours.

In fishing the rig was much favoured for its power, ability to sail well to windward, and manoeuvrability. Indeed, there were cutter-rigged fishing boats of all sorts and sizes – from small inshore fishers and dredgers to large offshore trawlers. From the late 1700s cutters were to be found sailing off all Britain's coasts and were used for trawling fish and shrimp, dredging oysters and mussels, stowboat-netting sprats, longlining cod, and more. The rig was popular, too, in the fishing fleets of Holland, Germany, race of 1926 and the Fastnet race of 1925, '28, and '30; more than 90 years old, she is still sailing. In Scandinavia Colin Archer – famous for his ketch-rigged rescue boats – also designed several cutter-rigged pilot boats.

In America, the predominance of the schooner and sloop rigs in working craft led to those sail plans (albeit vastly exaggerated) being adapted to their yachts; in Britain the propensity for the cutter rig had a similar result. Indeed, in the early 1800s British racing yachts resembled the revenue cutters of the day and were almost exclusively cutter-rigged and large. As competition grew, so did sail areas and hull sizes, until the mid 1830s when developments were getting out of hand and size was often restricted to under 75 tons. Yacht racing had become fairly organized by the 1840s with a season that started in the Thames and ended in the West Country, and the cutter was all-dominating. New technologies and sail-design were constantly being tested: in the mid 1860s on downwind legs *Niobe* set a triangular, boomed-out sail (it later became known as a 'spinnaker' – a corruption of *Sphynx*, the name of another yacht that followed *Niobe*'s example); in the 1870s steel wire was introduced for standing rigging and cotton replaced flax for sails.

At last, in 1881, the cutter made inroads in American yachting when G L Watson's *Madge*, designed and built in Britain in 1879, was shipped to New York and won six out of seven races against the local centreboard sloops. In response American designers created the 'compromise sloop': a rig comprising a large gaff mainsail and two headsails but with a fixed bowsprit shorter than was then typical on the British cutter. Within ten years both countries were sailing such yachts and the type reached its ultimate form with Nathanael Herreshoff's 1903 America's Cup winner *Reliance*. By the 1920s the trend was fading and the single-headsail sloop rig with jib-headed mainsail was fast becoming the most popular racing rig on both sides of the Atlantic.

The cutter has, nevertheless, hung on in cruising yachts, particularly for ocean voyaging, where a snug mainsail and the smaller headsails offer more versatility and are more easily handled by a small crew.

The 152ft LOA yacht *Lulworth* was built in 1920 to compete in the 'big class'. Her gaff-cutter sail plan – once the most popular for large British racing yachts – was already being superseded by the 'bermudan' jib-headed cutter or sloop plan.

CHAPTER 8

The Ketch

Favoured by European navies in the eighteenth century for use on bomb vessels, and in early colonial America for off-shore fishing, the ketch rig fell out of favour in the United States for all but small open boats, but re-emerged in British and Baltic waters to become the most common fore-and-aft rig in coastal trade and fishing.

DEFINITION

In its earliest definition the term 'ketch' referred to a 'full-rigged ship without a foremast' but for the last two centuries has described a two-masted vessel with the mainmast forward and taller than the mizzen, which is stepped forward of the rudder post. Initially square-rigged the type evolved into a fully fore-and-aft rig although some ketches

did still carry square main topsails into the very last days of commercial sail. In British and Baltic waters the commercial ketch became, almost exclusively, gaff-rigged on both masts with jib-headed topsails and multiple head-sails, while the small inshore ketches of the eastern United States and the Great Lakes were typically sprit-rigged, often with no headsail or, occasionally, one unstayed jib. In the modern era the ketch rig has been used on cruising yachts with gaff or bermudan sails on both masts, or with a wish-bone mainsail and mizzen staysail.

HISTORY

The ketch was not a popular naval rig and yet it was perhaps the French Navy of 1682 that first developed the type. The ketch-rigged bomb vessel was specifically designed to carry heavy mortars for shore bombardment and, for that purpose, its mainmast - with square course, topsail, and topgallant - was stepped nearly amidships; the mizzen had a crossjack and topsail above a lateen sail. Staysails were set and a spritsail was carried beneath the bowsprit, but the headsails were all removed during firing and, to with-stand the heat of bombardment, the forestay was of chain. By positioning the mainmast so far aft the bomb ketch had an uncluttered foredeck where two fixed mortars could be located - aim was taken by anchoring and warping the vessel into position or by backing sail. The Royal Navy fol-lowed the French in 1687 with the launching of the bomb ketch *Salamander*. From the 1720s the ketch also set a gaff spanker on the mainmast, but by the mid 1700s the revolv-ing mortar had been invented, allowing the guns to be aimed independent of the carrying vessel. Thereafter the ketch was quickly dropped in favour of the full-rigged ship.

Lowering the main topsail (with some difficulty perhaps) on the trading ketch *Ceres*. *Ceres* was built in 1811 for the fresh fruit trade between Spain and London, and worked for 125 years. (*H Oliver Hill*)

RIGHT One of the last Brixham trawlers to be built for sail, *Provident* is a typical 'mule' with powerful gaff-ketch rig. She was built in 1924 and fished for six years with a crew of three men and a boy. She is currently used for sail training by the Island Cruising Club, Salcombe, Devon, and is a designated vessel on the UK's National Register of Historic Vessels. (Nigel Pert)

In his book *Architectura Navalis Mercatoria*, published in 1768, F H Chapman identifies five different types of ketch. The nearest equivalent to the ketch that would emerge in northern Europe a century later was the 'Galleass used in the Baltic' – a vessel with two boomed, loose-footed gaff sails, one square main topsail, three headsails, one stayed, two flying. The others were the 'Ketch-yacht used in the Baltic' (two boomed loose-footed gaff sails, square main topgallant, topsail, and course, two flying headsails); the 'ketch' (two small gaff sails, a square mizzen topsail, main topsail and topgallant, one stayed and two flying headsails); the 'Dutch hoy' (lateen mizzen, square main course, and upper and lower topsails, two flying headsails); the 'Dogger' (boomed loose-footed gaff mizzen, boomless gaff mainsail, raked main topmast with square upper and lower topsails, four headsails, one stayed, three flying).

By the end of the eighteenth century the square-rigged ketch had all but faded into history. The fore-and-aft rig that replaced it and gained popularity around Britain and the Baltic was a development of the early square-rigged versions but also, perhaps, of trading cutters and sloops, which often set a small mizzen right in the stern. Whatever the route of evolution, from the mid 1800s the gaff-rigged ketch was the vessel of choice for Britain's coastal trade and the rapidly developing trawl fishing of the North Sea.

Through the nineteenth century, despite the advances of technology – a growing rail network and steam-powered shipping – the small sailing trader held its own around

Though a relatively simple two-masted rig, the ketch has nevertheless seen substantial change from its earliest beginnings.
1 A French invention, the bomb ketch (this one from 1679) stepped its mainmast well aft to keep the foredeck clear for heavy mortars. Note the lateen-rigged mizzen.
2 A later bomb ketch of the mid 1700s. Here the lateen mizzen has been replaced by a gaff trysail and a flying jib has been added.
3 The Dutch hoy of similar era is interesting for the pole mainmast; she has no mizzen topsail and, although the lateen sail has gone, the yard has been retained. Note, also, that the mainmast is stepped further forward – *ie* this is *not* a bomb ketch.
4 The Baltic ketch of the 1760s has a true gaff trysail on the mizzen and also a trysail on the main mast.
5 By the nineteenth century the Baltic ketch rig has become truly fore-and-aft although a square main course could be set in light weather, especially when running downwind.
6 A very similar nineteenth-century example, although note the lug mizzen topsail and the mainmast stepped further forward.
7–10 Never so popular in America (at least in the public consciousness) the ketch rig was nevertheless to be found, albeit under different names and most typically on small inshore fishing craft as (**7**) the Noman's Land boat, with spritsails and no headsails; (**8**) the Mackinaw boat (sometimes called Mackinaw ketch); (**9**) the Chesapeake Bay log canoe, with its well-raked masts and twin spritsails; and (**10**) the Chesapeake Bay bugeye also with raked masts but jib-headed sails.
11 The ketch rig is popular amongst modern cruising yachtsmen, particularly for its versatility when reducing sail – a well-balanced modern ketch will perform well under mizzen and staysail.

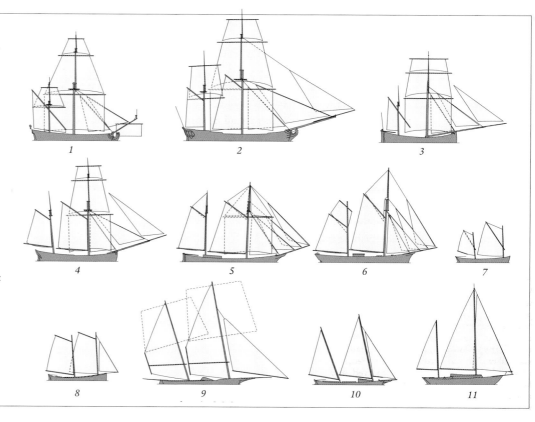

1

2

3

4

5

6

7

8

9

10

11

Britain's coasts, and the fore-and-aft rigs of schooners and ketches were favoured for their low maintenance and crew costs, good windward abilities, and manoeuvrability in crowded harbours and rivers. Trading ketches ranged in size from 30 to 150 tons but the majority was between 60 and 100 tons. In the early years they carried square topsails and, occasionally, large squaresails beneath the yard for downwind sailing, but by the 1850s most, if not all, square-sails had been taken off. The traders had standing bowsprits with headsails hanked to stays and some even had fully rigged jibbooms but these were not common.

As with so many mercantile rigs, there were regional differences in ketch sail plans but variety of hull shape was more marked – in the West hulls were typically deep-draughted, clipper-bowed, had modest counter sterns and graceful sheers; to the East the influence of shoal harbours and shallow estuaries led to more flat-bottomed, square-sided, shallow-draughted hulls that could work off beaches and up muddy creeks. Most distinct of all on the east coast were the Thames barges (see p.64) and from these developed the 'boomie' – a Thames barge hull whose sails were rigged with gaffs and booms instead of sprits – and the 'leeboard ketch' – a hybrid of the boomie and the trading ketch, which set a standard gaff-ketch rig on a hull with hard-chine mid-section and flat run, but with finer ends than the boomie, a moderate counter, short clipper bow, and higher bulwarks; the result was a combination of the most useful features of each type and, when afloat, the only distinguishing features were its leeboards.

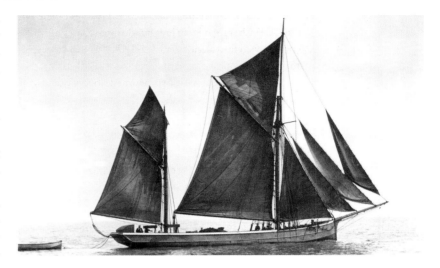

The last surviving ketches in the British trading fleet continued to work well into the twentieth century – the 97-ton *Irene* carried cargoes as late as 1939. In Denmark wooden trading ketches were still being built in the late 1940s, and in Finland wooden motor ketches were built for the south-coast aggregate trade even in the 1960s. Denmark's fleet finally collapsed in the 1960s in the face of rising costs of labour and maintenance, the construction of bridges between the country's islands, and the increased use of roll-on-roll-off ferries.

The ketch rig was not adopted into Britain's fishing fleets until the second half of the nineteenth century. As the herring fisheries of the north and east coasts went further

Well-laden, the British trading ketch *Grovehill* carries full sail including multiple headsails on a fixed bowsprit, jib-headed main topsail and lug mizzen topsail.

Henrietta, built in Cornwall in 1898, is a typical West Country trading ketch of her era. Her rig is workmanlike rather than extreme, but still offers great possibilities of sail combination. Her first 'reef' would be to lower the flying jib, then the outer jib or topsail, the mainsail could then be reefed, the jib lowered, the mizzen reefed, the staysail reefed, the mizzen double-reefed, ultimately the mainsail could be lowered, and the ketch would still be balanced under double-reefed mizzen and staysail – although to resort to this would signify very heavy conditions.

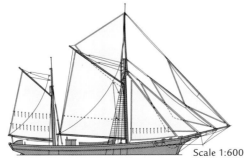

Scale 1:600

Scale 1:600

Built twenty-two years later for trawling on the East Coast, *Master Hand* is remarkably similar but perhaps more powerful with topsails on both masts, fewer headsails, but gear for deep reefs in both main and mizzen. Note, also, the mizzen topmast staysail.

THE THAMES BARGE

With its diminutive mizzen set well aft the rig of the Thames barge is often described as yawl but, with the transom-hung rudder abaft the mizzen, the rig is technically ketch. The type is first recorded by Chapman in his 1768 edition of *Architectura Navalis Mercatoria* where he shows a drawing of a sailing barge with boomless sprit mainsail and small foresail to the stem; the barge is 56ft long and was used for transporting chalk from the pits of Kent to London and Essex. Some seventy years later the rig had developed to include a topmast carrying a large jib-headed topsail, a tiny sprit mizzen, and sometimes a bowsprit. Barge racing began in the Thames estuary in the 1860s and at the same time larger barges were developed for seagoing trades; these set a much bigger mizzen carried further forward, and from time to time the sprit mainsail was replaced with a gaff sail – this last development led to the type being known as a 'boomy'.

The rig of the Thames barge is simple and could be handled – it was sometimes said – by one man and a boy, and yet the running rigging permitted many variations of sail set; it has been said that there are more control lines on a Thames barge's mainsail than on the most advanced of today's racing yachts. The mainsail has no halyard but is bent on before the mast is stepped. At the peak a loop is attached to the end of the sprit while the throat is held to the mast by an iron collar shackled to the sail. The luff is hanked to a jackstay that runs down the aft side of the mast. The mainsheet is attached to the leech in three places – at the clew and then twice above it at intervals of a few feet – thus the sail is flattened as it is sheeted in and the loads are spread around the canvas. There

Cambria, a typical large coasting Thames barge with sprit mainsail and gaff mizzen sail (in her earlier days she carried a spritsail on the mizzen), sailing with her bowsprit raised as she leaves (or approaches) harbour in the 1960s. Launched in 1906 she carried cargo under sail until 1970 and is currently being restored. (David MacGregor)

are no reef lines and as the sail cannot be lowered in the usual manner it is brailed up to the mast and sprit to reduce the area. The headsail is self tending, attached at its clew to a traveller mounted across the foredeck; there is a jib topsail (known by bargemen as the staysail), and a jib that can be hauled out along the bowsprit where it is set either flying or on a stay tensioned with a winch at the mast. The mizzen has a boomed spritsail sheeted to the aft upper corner of the rudder blade.

Barges continued to carry bulk cargoes in the Thames estuary region into the second half of the 1900s but inevitably in diminishing numbers. Today, though none carries commercial cargo, there are a number of restored barges used for charter and racing in the estuary and along the southeast coast of England.

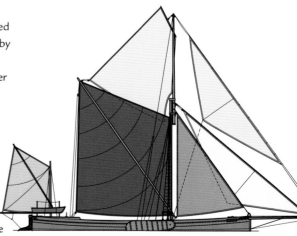

The Thames barge.   Scale 1:500

offshore so seaworthiness became of increasing importance. For distant trawling the previously favoured luggers (see p.85) were superseded by the gaff-rigged ketches, which proved more manoeuvrable and easier to handle by a small crew. As the trawl fishery grew so did the boats: where trawlers of 45ft had once been the norm, by the 1870s the popular length had grown to approximately 75ft and, like the luggers before them, the smaller single-masted cutters (see p.54) were replaced by larger ketches.

In the southwest the move from lugger to ketch came later but here, too, by the late 1800s the rig was almost universal for offshore fishing. Most famous today are the Brixham trawlers built from the 1880s to the mid 1920s and divided into two groups: over and under 40 tons; the smaller being known locally as 'mules'. On both types the rig had a pronounced forward rake and loose-footed sails were set on both main and mizzen; two working headsails were set (one stayed, one flying) and a light-weather flying jib could also be carried. Unlike the trading ketches, the trawlers had a running bowsprit that could be housed on deck. These large vessels could be worked by small crews of four – often including one or even two boys.

While the ketch rig made inroads into offshore trading and fishing in northern Europe, in the United States and Canada it was almost exclusively seen on small open boats working inshore. Typical were the eighteenth- and nineteenth-century fishing boats off the Massachusetts coast around Cape Cod and the islands of Martha's Vineyard, Nantucket, and Noman's Land. These small boats – rarely more than 25ft in length – set two spritsails of equal or near-equal height (in schooner-style, the forward was known as the 'foresail' and the after as the 'mainsail'); with the foresail stepped far forward and no bowsprit, they carried neither staysail nor jib. The quaintly named Block Island Cowhorn had jib-headed sails and no headsail while some square-sterned Hampton boats of New Hampshire and Maine, set a large foresail that overlapped the smaller mainsail (both were sprit-rigged), and had a jib tacked down to a removable bowsprit. All these boats could be sailed and rowed by one or two men.

Similar rigs were found on the Great Lakes where the largest of the types, the Huron and the Mackinaw boats, could be gaff rigged (the latter also set a jib). Some sharpies and sharpie skiffs were also ketch rigged, as were the Chesapeake Bay log canoes and bugeyes. Later log canoes had two aft-raked unstayed masts carrying jib-headed sails whose leech ended in a vertical club to which a horizontal sprit was fastened; the bugeyes had two aft-raked stayed masts with jib-headed sails; both types had a single headsail.

In the 1870s the amateur designer Ralph Munro created some interesting cruisers based on Florida sharpies. Sam

Crocker of Manchester, Massachusetts, working from 1915 to 1960, revived the type, and most famously L. Francis Herreshoff was an advocate of the rig on both small and large cruising yachts – *Ticonderoga*, the 72ft ketch built in 1936, was one of his most successful designs. In Britain the bermudan ketch has proved more popular with amateur yachtsmen, especially for cruising: what may be lost in speed is gained in ease of sail handling. *Suhaili*, the first yacht to make a non-stop single-handed circumnavigation of the world (1968), was a 32ft ketch.

The trading ketch *Elizabeth* leaving Bude in north Cornwall. She has a relatively simple rig with loose-footed gaff sails, only two headsails – the jib being tacked to a running bowsprit – a lug topsail on the main, and a jib-headed topsail on the mizzen.

C H A P T E R

The Yawl

Rarely seen in working vessels the two-masted yawl rig is a late arrival, gaining favour in yachts and small sailing boats from the late 1800s.

DEFINITION

The early use of the word 'yawl' referred to a hull rather than its rig – in the Royal Navy the yawl was a smaller ship's boat; in mercantile and fishing fleets, yawls were typically inshore open boats, but with diverse rigs. From time to time boats were converted from other rigs to a sail plan that might, today, be described as 'yawl rigged' but which in earlier times would more usually be known as 'dandy-rigged' – where a large mainsail was cut down for ease of handling and a small mizzen mast was stepped far aft to re-establish sail balance. In America the term 'yawlboat' is still used for a small open boat used in support of a larger vessel.

Today the term 'yawl' refers specifically to a two-masted rig where the mizzen mast is stepped abaft the rudder post. The mainsail can be gaff or jib-headed and although the mizzen was typically a standing lug in its earliest days it,

---

1–2 Although predominantly a yachting rig, the yawl was to be found on some working boats such as (**1**) the Dunkerque fishing boats of the late nineteenth and early twentieth centuries and (**2**) the larger Grimsby cod smacks of the same era. Both types set gaff-rigged mainsails, lug-rigged main topsail, staysail, and jib (the Grimsby boat also had a flying jib), but where the French boat's mizzen sail was lug-rigged, that of the British boat was gaff-rigged.
3–6 Most popular as a small-boat rig at the turn of the twentieth century, the yawl found favour with 'everyman' sailors on both sides of the Atlantic. Examples include (**3**) the Roslyn yawl of the late 1870s with jib-headed sprit mizzen, high-peaked gaff mainsail, and jib;

(**4**) *Vagabond*, an American canoe yawl with sprit-rigged mizzen sail and sliding gunter mainsail (see Luggers, p.85); (**5**) *Viking*, a more substantial British canoe yawl; and (**6**) *Wenda* of 1899 with gunter-rigged mizzen and standing-lug-rigged mainsail.
7 Of similar vintage, *Clara* is a cat-yawl, her mainmast stepped right in the eyes of the boat, her two sails fully-battened, and with a sprit to their peaks.
8 There were also yawl-rigged gentleman's yachts – especially in Britain – in the second half of the nineteenth century, like the Fife-designed *Fairlie* of 1868 – note how much smaller the mizzen sail is when compared to the ketch rigs of the previous chapter.

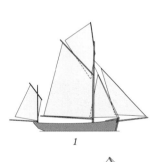

1

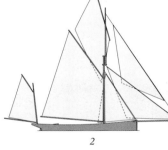

2

3

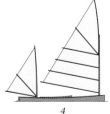

4

5

6

7

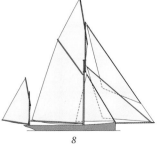

8

Inspired by John MacGregor and his yawl, the *Rob Roy* (see p.71), Empson Edward Middleton commissioned a similar 21ft gaff-and-standing-lug yawl, the *Kate*, in which he circumnavigated Britain, singlehanded, in the summer of 1869.

too, has evolved to be typically gaff or jib-headed. Yawls often set two headsails, in cutter fashion, although this is not a prerequisite of the type.

(It should be noted that the yawl rig is sometimes defined not by the mizzen mast's position but in terms of sail size – *ie* if the mizzen is 'much smaller' than the mainsail, then some will describe the rig as a yawl. Thus, boats such as the Thames barge (see p.64) and, indeed, the Salcombe Yawl are sometimes said to be 'yawls' even though the rudder is transom-hung and, therefore, aft of the mizzen.)

HISTORY

The origins of the yawl rig are obscure but it almost certainly grew out of the dandy rig of coastal British craft in the early nineteenth century. Never prolific in working fleets, the herring drifters of Dunkerque gradually evolved from lug rigs to the yawl rig in the late 1800s and early 1900s. But it was in pleasure sailing that the yawl was most keenly developed. By the mid 1800s it was finding favour in yachts – several of which were converted from cutter rigs – and as the century progressed and yacht design was increasingly influenced by

LEFT 'Yawl on the Port Tack' by Captain James Haughton Forrest, *c.*1880.
Although the cutter rig was perhaps more typical of British gentleman's yachts of her day, Forrest's yawl would not have been an unfamiliar sight. She sets a standing lug mizzen, gaff mainsail, lug topsail, staysail, and jib. Of interest is the yard on the mainmast; it might be used for a downwind sail. (Royal Exchange Art Gallery, London)

RIGHT The Concordia yawl, designed by Waldo Howland and C Raymond Hunt in 1938, is the archetypal classic cruising yawl of the twentieth century. Some 103 were built between 1938 and 1966 making it the largest class of wooden one-design yachts ever. All 103 survive. (Jenny Bennett)

rating rules the yawl grew in popularity for larger yachts. The first large racer to be designed and built as a yawl was the 112-ton *Ursuline* launched in Lymington in 1858; seven years later the 222-ton *Lufra*, built in Cowes, was a successful racer that inspired several new yawls built to compete against the schooners of the 1860s and '70s. A rating change in the 1880s witnessed a temporary decline in yawl-rigged yachts but the type re-emerged in the 1890s (again thanks to a rule change) when many of the large cutters reduced their main booms and stepped mizzens. The William Fifes

of Fairlie were keen promoters of the rig – among the later great yawls of the prewar era was the Fife-designed *Sumurun* of 1914) – as were Summers and Payne of Southampton – their 80ft *Leander* won the King's Cup in 1902.

But the yawl was not just a rig for the great racers, in Britain it also won favour with cruising yachtsmen for small craft often designed for singlehanded sailing, the great advantage of the rig being its adaptability for short-handed crews. Two of the prime early supporters were John MacGregor and R T McMullen, both of whom extensively

A clinker-built beach yawl on England's south coast poses for the camera. The yawl is a perfect rig for carrying passengers – the boomless mainsail is no threat to the heads of the unknowing, and the split rig offers the versatility to cope with various wind strengths without compromising steerage.

Two famous yawls.

The 21ft *Rob Roy*, built for John MacGregor of London in 1867, in which he cruised, single-handed from London to Paris and back via le Havre and the Isle of Wight. Her rig – standing-lug mizzen, gaff-rigged mainsail, and jib is not extravagant but would have well-suited MacGregor's solitary purposes.

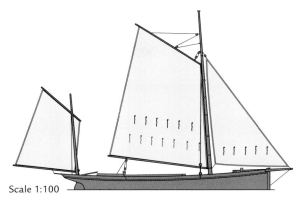

Scale 1:100

Dorade, designed by Olin Stephens in 1930, bucked the trend in American ocean-racing which, in the 1920s, had still favoured the schooner rig. Today her rig would be described as a conventional bermudan (or jib-headed) yawl, with multiple headsails – staysail, jib, flying jib. She had no engine and her designer praised the mizzen sail for giving added steerage in confined waters.

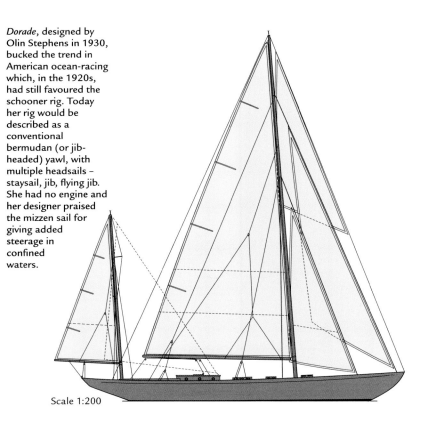

Scale 1:200

cruised and wrote of their experiences – MacGregor published *Sailing alone in the Yawl Rob Roy* in which he told of sailing single-handed from the Thames to Paris in the 21ft *Rob Roy* built in 1867, and in *Down Channel* McMullen wrote of cruises he made in *Orion*, a cutter converted to yawl in 1873. MacGregor had also popularised sailing canoes when, in the 1860s, he built a series of small canoes in which he paddled and sailed across Europe and Egypt. In 1865 he founded the Royal Canoe Club, which went on to have branches on the Thames, Mersey, and Humber (and to inspire the New York Canoe Club). Through their auspices the canoe yawl grew from paddling boat to recognised small cruising type, many of which were drawn by George Holmes and, later, Albert Strange.

On the east coast of America the yawl rig was virtually unknown before the 1880s although in San Francisco it was introduced by C H Harrison who brought a small yawl from England in 1840. Harrison became the commodore of the San Francisco Yacht Club and, perhaps because of his influence, the yawl rig was popular among club members into the 1870s. On the east coast its rise can be traced to two sources. Here the first recorded yawl is thought to have been the 23ft *Coquette*, built in Britain before 1868 and brought to America in 1878 by Henry Eaton. Concurrently, Thomas Clapham developed the Connecticut oyster sharpie to a yawl-rigged 'yacht' and thence to the type known as the Nonpareil (or Roslyn) model, which had a jib-headed mizzen, high-peaked gaff mainsail, and two headsails. In the 1880s the yachting writer C P Kunhardt took up the cause and championed the rig for small yachts and singlehanding. In time, many famous American designers – among them Herreshoff, William Atkin, and John Alden – would create cruising yawls.

Several famous long-distance yachts have been yawl-rigged: Joshua Slocum's *Spray*, Thomas Fleming Day's *Sea Bird*, Arthur Payne's 1882 design, *Amaryllis*, which circumnavigated in 1922–23. And one of the most famous of all twentieth-century racing yachts, *Dorade*, designed by Olin Stephens in 1930 and described by many as the fore-runner of the modern ocean racer, was a 52ft, bermudan yawl.

10

The Schooner

Built for speed and efficiency, the schooner rig first emerged in Europe but became popular on both sides of the Atlantic for trade and fishing. Of all the commercial rigs it has survived in greatest numbers, especially in North America and today is still favoured on many larger cruising yachts.

DEFINITION

When first coined, the term schooner applied to a two-masted vessel, fore-and-aft rigged on both, with square topsails on both. As the type developed, so did the variety of sail plans, but the essentials continued to be two or more masts of equal height (or, in the case of the two-masters, with a foremast shorter than the main), fore-and-aft-rigged on all, with or without topsails, which could be square or jib-headed. At the peak of commercial development the schooners of Europe continued to set square topsails on the foremast and there the one-word term 'schooner' signified this; a European schooner without squaresails came to be described as a 'fore-and-aft schooner'. Conversely, in America the schooner quickly developed without squaresails and thus, where square topsails were carried the vessel would be called a 'topsail schooner'.

Within these broader definitions there are more precise terms: bald-headed schooner (no topsails of any kind); two-topsail or main-topsail schooner (carries squaresails on the topmasts of both fore- and mainmasts); topgallant schooner (carries two topsails and a topgallant on the foremast); sharpie schooner (two-masted with jib-headed sails on both, clewed out by horizontal sprits; latterly developed into the wishbone schooner rig seen on modern cruising yachts); tern schooner (three-masted, fore-and-aft schooner whose masts are all of equal height); schooner ketch (three-

1 An American schooner of 1780, *Berbice* shows slightly aft-raked masts and only fore-and-aft sails on her mainmast – both familiar features of later American fast schooners.

2 Both British and American shallops of the mid 1700s were typically rigged with two sails of near equal size, the foremast being stepped as far forward as possible. In the British variation (seen here from 1806) a bowsprit and large jib were also set.

3 A Virginia pilot of about 1800, this schooner's mast rake looks distinctly American although the short gaffs are reminiscent of Dutch craft; the large overlapping main topmast staysail is of interest.

4–5 The ballahou schooners of Bermuda, *c*1800, though native, set gaff-rigged sails – the main boomed but loose-footed, the foresail boomless and overlapping – while other later schooners (1820–50) like the three-masted variation shown here (**5**), carried jib-headed sails, which were more efficient to windward.

6 Jib-headed schooners were not only to be found in Bermuda – many of the Levant (Mediterranean) schooners of the late nineteenth and early twentieth centuries set such sails. Note the large overlapping foresail and long jib-boom.

7–8 Schooners were to be seen throughout North America and on variously sized craft from small inshore open boats, to Nova Scotian Tancook Whalers (**7**) of the late nineteenth century, which ranged in size from 24ft to 50ft (note the boomed self-tacking staysail and boomless overlapping foresail), to the handsome Grand Banks schooners like *Arethusa* (**8**) a 127ft 3in auxiliary fishing schooner built in 1907.

9 *Margaret Haskell* of 1904 is large but carries the typical fore-and-aft rig of the American coastal trading schooner of the late nineteenth early twentieth centuries. All her masts are of equal height.

10 Conventionally, the staysail schooner set all canvas (except the aftermost sail) from the vessel's stays. This hybrid auxiliary schooner sets substantial sails on her stays *but* the luffs of the fore- and mainsails are bent to their masts and clewed out to the stay.

11 The four-masted topsail schooner was not common except in Scandinavia. *Helga* was typical in most respects except for her square foresail, which is reminiscent of a barquentine rig.

masted schooner whose mizzen is considerably shorter than the other two masts); staysail schooner (with the exception of the main all sails are set on stays, thus infilling the space between the masts and the deck – the rig saves weight aloft and is said to be more efficient than the traditional schooner); modern bermudan schooner (mainsail is bermudan – *ie* jib-headed – foresail may be bermudan or gaff).

Other terms related as much to place or hull-shape as to rig. Space does not allow mention of all types but, for example, the pinky schooner was a two-masted inshore fishing schooner from New England with a pronounced sheer, sharp stern, and narrow transom; the Chebacco dogbody was similar but fuller bodied and with a square stern; its foremast was stepped in the eyes of the boat and there was no bowsprit or headsail. The ballahou schooner was a native of Bermuda that set two narrow short-headed gaff

ABOVE The two-masted topsail schooner *My Lady* sailing under full rig – including lug main topsail – off Holyhead in 1932.

LEFT The fore-and-aft schooner *Elizabeth Drew*. Her sails have seen better days – the multiple patches on the mainsail are evidence of the chafing topping lift. This photograph clearly shows the typical two-halyard set up for hoisting the gaff sails.

sails as seen on traditional Dutch craft, while the Bermudian gaff schooner was three-masted with a single headsail, and the Bermudian schooner was three-masted with jib-headed sails throughout. The San Francisco schooner-scow had a two-masted schooner rig on a shallow-draught, flat-bottomed hull with centreboard, while the pungy schooner of Chesapeake Bay was also two-masted but had a deep keel and no centreboard. Away from American coasts the European fruit schooners were typically two-masted with square fore topsails and topgallant, and raked masts, while

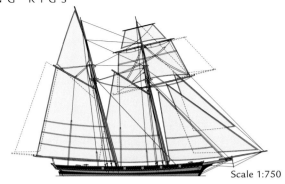

LEFT *Pride of Baltimore II* carries the typical rig of a Baltimore schooner of the early 1800s. Of particular note are the raked masts, large gaff-rigged fore- and main-sails, narrow jib-headed main topsail, and double fore topsails complete with studding sail on the lower. It is a dramatic rig designed for speed.

Scale 1:750

BELOW AND OPPOSITE The enormous *Thomas W. Lawson* was the only seven-masted vessel ever launched. The nomenclature of her masts was always a matter for discussion, even amongst those who sailed her. However, according to Captain Archie Horka in the book *Medley of Mast and Sail* edited by Alex Hurst, for five-masted schooners the accepted names (from bow to stern) were: fore, main, mizzen, jigger, spanker; and for six-masted schooners: fore, main, mizzen, jigger, driver, spanker; so for seven masters an acceptable standard could be fore, main, mizzen, jigger, driver, pusher, spanker. What is a known fact is that all the masts on *Thomas W. Lawson* were of equal height and the five inner gaff sails of equal proportions, as were their topsails and staysails.

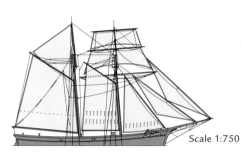

Scale 1:750

LEFT Another two-masted topsail schooner, *Isabella*, built in northeast England in 1892, carries an altogether more workmanlike rig than the Baltimore version, but nevertheless there are similarities from the relative sail proportions, to the angle of the gaffs and the number of working sails. However, built for trade, not privateering, *Isabella*'s rig – especially the foresail which does not overlap – would be more easily handled by a short-handed crew.

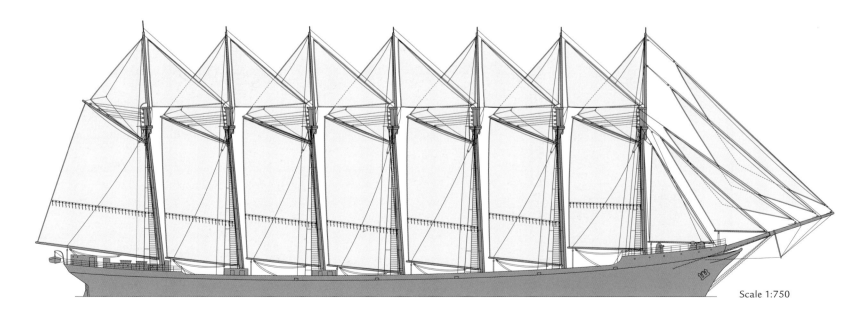

Scale 1:750

the Levant schooner of the eastern Mediterranean set jib-headed sails on two well-raked masts, three headsails above a distinctive hull with square stern, pronounced sheer, and flared bow.

HISTORY

Exactly where or when the schooner first appeared is much debated but it is known to have existed on balsa rafts on the South American Pacific coast in the early 1500s. In Europe it first emerged on Dutch leisure craft in the 1600s. By the late 1600s it had crossed the North Sea to England: in 1695 King William III launched the two-masted gaff-rigged yacht *Royal Transport*. Soon the rig was to be found on both merchant and navy vessels, and by the early 1700s had appeared in North America on small naval 'sloops', shallops, and fishing boats. By the mid 1730s it was an established rig and by the 1740s at least twenty-two American privateers were schooner-rigged.

Built in 1902 she worked first in the coal trade and then in oil. Being relatively under-canvassed she was never thought beautiful, and it is questionable if she even paid for the cost of her build. She had much steam-assist gear and could be crewed by just sixteen men.

The history of the schooner is, essentially, a story of two halves: the British and European schooner, and the American schooner. In North America the schooner swiftly became the rig of choice for anything from small inshore fishing boats, to coastal cargo carriers, to ocean-going traders. But in Britain and northern Europe, it remained something of a rarity until the early 1800s. Some schooners were adopted into the Royal Navy but for the most part these were not British built but were, rather, purchased or later captured from the Americans. Nevertheless, despite its late start, once the schooner had been adopted by the British merchant fleets it made rapid and widespread progress: by the 1860s the schooner was the most common rig in British trade.

For the most part the British schooner was a relatively small vessel. The largest was the 2084-ton *Earl of Aberdeen* built in 1890, but she was unusual – the more common range was between 50 and 200 tons (although some were as small as 40 tons) and nearly all were built of wood. Rigs varied in their detail (there were regional differences and the rig did evolve over time) but generally the British vessel was a two- or three-masted topsail schooner. The square-sails came in various combinations: single topsail and flying topgallant; single topsail and standing topgallant; two-masted with double topsails on both masts; three-masted with double topsails and standing topgallant, with flying topgallant on the fore. They were used in coastal and short-sea trades and saw their greatest evolutionary refinement pursuing the fresh-fruit trade of the mid 1800s. Employed in both Britain and Germany but principally British-built, the fruit schooner typically was about 100ft in length and of about 150 tons. They were designed to be fast and often plied a triangular route from their homeport west to the Grand Banks with salt; there they would take on cod, which would be salted down and delivered to southern Europe; thence fresh fruit would be sailed north to Germany, the Netherlands, Scandinavia, and Britain. Some British fruit schooners, especially of the south and west coasts, were employed in a simple there-and-back trade between Britain

LEFT Sailing in Puget Sound, Washington, the five-masted schooner *Bianca* sets a most unusual rig. In a following breeze she has triangular topsails set below yards on all but the mainmast, and upper topsails above the yards from the head of three masts – the yards appear to be inter-dependent with sheets running from yard arm to yard arm. In addition to the topsails and fore staysails, each mast has boomed, loose-footed, narrow, jib-headed lower sails all of which are set (except on the mainmast where the crew are either readying the sail for hoisting or furling it having just lowered it).

Placing the origin of the term is even less easy: popular myth suggests that the word was first used at Gloucester, Massachusetts, when, at the launching of a two-masted vessel in 1713 an onlooker was said to have exclaimed 'see how she scoons'; the builder responded: 'let her a scooner be!'. Fact or fiction, the term repeatedly appeared in print from the 1730s and was surely of American derivation. Eventually, it was officially recorded in William Falconer's 1769 *Universal Dictionary of the Marine*: 'a small vessel with two masts, whose main-sail and fore-sail are suspended from gaffs reaching from the mast towards the stern; and stretched out below by booms...'.

and the Mediterranean, the Azores, or the Canaries. Of similar size to the North Sea schooners, these 'clipper schooners' were deep-hulled and fine-lined, two-masted (with much rake) and set topsails and topgallants. Speed was of the essence. A record run for one such vessel in the 1840s was five days from the Azores to the Lizard – a voyage of some 1,100 miles. In 1869 *Elinor* sailed from London Bridge to the Azores and back in 17 days.

By the outbreak of World War I the schooner in Britain had had its day. Elsewhere in Europe it lingered on and where it did so four-masters became popular. In Denmark, for instance, fifty-one four-masted schooners were built between 1913 and 1924; most set single yards on the foremast and were otherwise fore-and-aft rigged. In Portugal two five-masters were built in 1919; in Germany five five-masters were built between 1921 and 1922, and in Italy there was even a concrete-hulled five-master launched in 1922.

While in Europe the schooner worked alongside many and diverse square-riggers and fore-and-afters, in North America the type became the single most important rig.

The earliest known records of schooners in America are from the early 1700s and by the middle of that century the rig had taken hold and was to be found on fishing boats, oyster dredgers, coastal cargo carriers, deep-water traders, pilot boats, and naval vessels. Its greatest advantages were its ability to sail close to the wind and the fact that it could be manned by a considerably smaller crew than any comparative square-rigger: what it lacked in power over long distance, it made up for in close-quarters speed and manoeuvrability. Its rise in popularity through a century that saw a decrease in almost all other types of sailing craft in America, was remarkable and, to quote maritime historian Howard Chapelle, 'by 1790, if not earlier, the schooner was the national rig of both the United States and Canada'.

The earliest known American schooners were built in Virginia, especially in the Chesapeake Bay area. They were typically two-masted with topsails on just the foremast or on both masts; their foresails were boomed, although later models preferred an overlapping boomless foresail. Con-

flict with Britain during the War of Independence saw a rapid development in the type – now the principal demand was for speed for privateering and blockade running. Extreme rigs and hulls were developed: very fine lines and low freeboard coupled with massive fore-and-aft sails, little

or no standing rigging, and quite extraordinary mast rake. Many of the experimental designs were first tried on small Virginia pilot boats, which, during the years of war, were sometimes pressed into transatlantic crossings in pursuit of British ships or European trading. By the turn of the century larger schooners were emerging, ranging in size from about 65ft to 95ft, but the so-called 'sharp' schooners continued to develop until, by the time of the War of 1812, the type had reached its peak, as exemplified by the radical Baltimore clippers – made famous by their daring exploits against British shipping and, in recent times, by the replicas *Pride of Baltimore*, and *Pride of Baltimore II*.

The 1329-ton *Thomas S. Dennison* was built by Dunn & Elliot of Thomaston, Maine, in 1900. Typical of the less extreme coastal schooners of her day, with four masts and tall topsails she would have been extremely able. Unlike the two-masted schooner sailing under her lee, her masts all appear to be of equal height – a common feature of larger American schooners.

LEFT Some rigs defied easy classification. *Carl Vinnen*, built in Germany in 1922, was a five-masted schooner with square topsails and topgallant on the fore and mizzen, and jib-headed topsails on the main, jigger, and driver; the term 'five-masted, two-topsail schooner' has been applied.

As the nineteenth century settled down into more peaceful times, existing American schooners were employed wherever there was a need for speed – particularly infamous were those in the slave and opium trades. But the rig was developed for all manner of vessels, none more renowned than the fishing schooners of New England, designed and built to fish for mackerel – shoals were chased down (often to windward) and surrounded with a purse seine net – or for exploiting the seemingly endless cod stocks on the Grand Banks off Newfoundland. Of all the schooners in

the fishing trades, the most famous were those that sailed 'downeast' from Massachusetts to the Banks, launched their deck-carried dories, salted down the catch in deep, dark holds, and sailed back, laden with tons of fish, for the markets of New England. And of these none was more famous than the Canadian designed and built *Bluenose*. She was launched in 1921 to be a fast racer but also a competitive 'salt banker' sailing twice a year between New England and the Banks, and once every winter, to the West Indies with a cargo of cod, returning north with a hold full

One of the most famous schooners of all time, *Bluenose*, launched in Canada, 1921, was renowned for her success as a racer but worked with the Grand Banks fishing fleets for nearly twenty years. Lost near Haiti in 1946, another schooner – *Bluenose II* – was built to the same lines and launched in 1964.

A small topsail schooner, *Rob Roy* of Cork. Note the forward bend in the main topmast, caused by the filling main topmast staysail – if the main topsail was raised the forward pull would be counteracted but the schooner might then overpressed. (W A Sharman)

of salt. She was both fast and powerful, displacing 285 tons, capable of loading 210 tons, and setting 10,970sq.ft of sail on two masts. Her overall length was 111ft 9in and both her mainmast and -boom were 81ft long.

Coastal trade grew through the 1800s as the eastern seaboard became increasingly populated and industrialised: coal was carried north from Virginia, ice south from Maine, cotton and tobacco north from the southern states, and all in schooners. In the first half of the nineteenth century virtually none was more than 150 tons and few had more than two masts; but by the late 1800s there were many schooners of more than 500 tons and they carried an increasing number of masts. Three-masters became

common in the 1830s and '40s but as cargo capacity became a greater requirement, so vessels grew in size and, in 1890, the first four-masted coasting schooner, the 250ft *William L. White*, was launched in Bath, Maine. More followed – mostly in the 180ft to 240ft range and typically fitted with centreboards to allow the vessels to sail into shoal harbours and onto beaches (centreboards were eventually removed to create more hold space and as port tug services became cheaper and more common). Curiously, steam power, the great threat of other fleets, helped the American schooner increase in size and competitiveness: steam winches and windlasses were introduced to assist small crews in raising sails, anchors, and spars – the first

One of a very few original two-masted American coasting schooners still sailing, the *Grace Bailey* was built in 1882 in Patchogue, New York. Bald-headed with a jib and self-tacking staysail, her mainmast is offset from the centreline to accommodate the centreboard trunk. (Jenny Bennett)

known steam windlass was fitted for this purpose on the 758-ton *Charles A. Briggs*, a three-master built in Bath, Maine, in 1879.

As the century drew to a close the size of the coasting schooner continued its relentless growth. The first five-master, the 1764-ton *Governor Ames*, was launched in 1888. Over the next thirty years some fifty-six five-masters were built – such as the 2400-ton *Nathaniel T. Palmer* in 1898 – and the last of the type, the 1512-ton *Edna Hoyt*, was launched in 1920 in Thomaston, Maine. Finally, there were the six-masters. Of the ten built, the first was *George W. Wells* launched in 1900 and followed the same year by the *Eleanor A. Percy*; the largest of the type, and indeed the largest of

all wooden schooners, was *Wyoming*, 3730 tons, 325ft 6in long, built in 1909. But seven years before her the even more remarkable *Thomas W. Lawson* had been launched in Quincy, Massachusetts. She was steel-hulled and, at 5218 tons, the largest schooner ever built. She stepped a unique seven masts, all of identical height: her steel lowers rising 135ft from keel to cap, the pine topmasts being 58ft. She had steam power for handling sails – halyards, sheets, and topping lifts – and to assist with her steering. Thanks to such technology she needed a crew of only sixteen men. She was lost while riding out a gale at anchor off the Scilly Isles, Cornwall, in 1907.

But even as the big schooners were being launched their

The six-masted fore-and-aft schooner *Myette* sets topmast staysails from each mast, and both the fore staysail and jib are boomed to be 'self-tacking'. (A Cromby)

days were numbered, motorisation was stealing their trade and with improved road and rail networks more and more goods were being transported overland. Nevertheless, a massive rise in cargo rates saw a temporary boom through World War I when many schooners changed hands for vastly inflated prices and carried war supplies across the Atlantic.

Despite the huge hull sizes that emerged at the end of their era schooners were generally smaller than many of their ocean-going counterparts and it is perhaps this more than anything that has ensured their survival in the world's sail-training and heritage fleets. Nowhere is this more true than in the United States where the vast majority of today's large sailing vessels are schooner-rigged, either original survivors or new-built replicas.

The rig has also lived on in leisure craft – where it first emerged four centuries ago. For more than 150 years it graced large racing yachts on both sides of the Atlantic and was much developed in its details by some of the world's greatest designers: Herreshoff, Fife, Burgess, Nicholson, Alden. Today, however, it is more commonly used for cruising than for racing.

Perhaps the most famous yacht of all time was the schooner-rigged yacht *America* launched in New York in 1851 and winner of that year's Hundred Guineas Cup competed for around the Isle of Wight, England. The trophy was renamed the America's Cup and was held by the Americans from then until 1983 – the world's longest unbroken record in any competitive sport.

CHAPTER 11

The Lugger

Favoured for open work boats and fishing boats, the lugger was popular throughout northern Europe, yet was not much favoured in America except in colonial naval and some earlier whaling boats. While lugsails may be used in various sail-plan configurations – sloop, ketch, yawl, etc – vessels setting such rigs are rarely so described. Thus, the 'lugger' is here given its own chapter. Today variations of the rig are used on small leisure boats and replicas.

DEFINITION

A lugger is any vessel that sets a lugsail – a four-sided sail whose head, bent to a yard, is shorter than the foot, and whose luff is shorter than the leech – for its principal sail. It may have one, two, or three masts, and while it usually has a lugsail on each mast, may have a jib-headed sail on the mizzen. The lugsail itself comes in a variety of forms: dipping, balance, standing, gunter and sliding gunter, settee, and split.

Despite its simplicity the lug rig gave rise to many subtle variations as can be seen here.

1–3 These first three drawings are all boats with dipping-lug sails. The Fifie from Scotland (1) has a high-peaked dipping-lug foresail on an aft-raking mast and a standing-lug mizzen on fore-raking mast. Although she does have a bowsprit and jib she could sail without. The New Orleans lugger (2) – the only successful lug-rigged working boat in North America – has a low-peaked dipping lugsail with vertical leading edge that would have had multiple reef points reaching up to more than half the height of the sail. The Sgoth of the Hebrides (3) has a high-peaked sail with a more angled leading edge; all three dipping lugsails would have been set on unstayed masts – the halyard acting as the windward shroud.

4 The split lug would seem an obvious departure from the dipping lug but lacked power and was not successful. The yard did not need to be dipped and the forward part of the sail was independently sheeted like a headsail.

5 The settee resembles the lateen and dipping lugsail but, in the manner of the balance lugsail, was not dipped.

6 The balance lug was not much used on working boats except for mizzen sails. However, it was popular in Britain in the late nineteenth century for small leisure boats and dinghies when it was often combined with a small jib.

7 The gunter-lug (seen here on a Sonder Class yacht of the early twentieth century) was a leisure-craft sail.

8-9 In recent years the lug rig has again become popular on small leisure boats and here the standing version has become the favourite either in its most simple form on small dinghies (8) or – as seen on the Nigel Irens-designed *Roxane* (9) – on more sophisticated cabin boats.

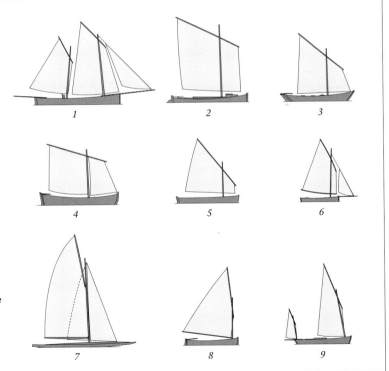

DIPPING LUGSAIL: A boomless sail whose yard extends forward of the mast; the foot is tacked down to a fitting on the centerline of the boat well forward of the mast. A powerful sail, it is set to the lee of the mast and thus must be brought around the mast (dipped), as the boat turns through the wind. Because of the additional work when tacking, the dipping lugsail is not suitable for confined waters or in work where frequent turns must be made. The mast is usually unstayed, the halyard being used as a windward shroud.

BALANCE LUGSAIL: Also sometimes known as a French lug, the balance lugsail is boomed. Both yard and boom extend forward of the mast, but less so than the dipping lugsail. The yard is not dipped and the sail remains set up on one side or the other, regardless of wind direction. The mast is usually unstayed.

STANDING LUGSAIL: Commonly used as a mizzen sail on working craft, and as the single sail on small boats, the standing lugsail may be boomed or boomless. Its yard is more peaked than that of either the dipping or balance lugsail, and extends forward of the mast but never more than about one third of its length. The tack is secured to the mast and, as with the balance lugsail, the yard is not dipped. The mast may be stayed but this is not usual, especially in small rigs.

GUNTER LUGSAIL: Similar to the standing lugsail but the yard is brought almost vertical, its heel held to the mast by jaws (as used for a gaff sail). The gunter lugsail is used on small pleasure craft. A variation is the sliding gunter where the yard is raised vertically against and extends well above the mast, being held in position by two travellers that slide up and down the mast. It is an efficient rig for small boats where the yard is not unmanageably long.

SETTEE SAIL: This is a rare form of the lugsail and is best described as a combination of a lateen and a dipping

LEFT *Mary Ann*, a fishing boat from Arbroath, Scotland. From the angle of the shot it is hard to say whether she is a zulu or fifie. However, the presence of a bumkin extending beyond the stern does suggest a mizzen, which would have been usual on such a boat. What is less usual is the standing lugsail: most boats of this size and era – late nineteenth, early twentieth century – would have been rigged with dipping lugsails. (Smith, Arbroath, Scotland)

lugsail; its luff is very short and both yard and boom extend far forward of the mast.

SPLIT LUGSAIL: Also rare, the split lugsail was an attempt to profit from the power of the dipping lugsail but do away with the disadvantage of having to dip the yard. The head of the sail is bent to the yard but the sail is split vertically in way of the mast; aft of the mast it is tacked to the mast and handled as a boomless standing lugsail, forward of the mast it is tacked down in the bow of the boat, has two sheets, and is controlled like a jib.

HISTORY

The lugsail is undoubtedly ancient in its concept, being used in the far and middle east for millennia (in China and other Asiatic nations it took the form of fully-battened sails, while in Arabic societies it took the form of the lateen sail – see p.89), yet it did not come into general use in northern European waters until at least the early seventeenth century. In these regions it is hard to pinpoint the exact origin of the lugsail; it is possible that the type slowly infiltrated from the south, a development of the lateen sail, but it is just as possible that it evolved locally, from the squaresail; indeed, it is not a big stretch of the imagination to consider twisting a square main course and tilting its yard to create a dipping lugsail. Whatever its evolution, by the late eighteenth/early nineteenth centuries the lugsail was a common sight around many European coasts.

The French naval lugger, capable of sailing well to windward and with immense power off the wind was comparative to the contemporary British cutter or the American schooner. Its tall, three-masted rig carried high-peaked dipping lugsails on the fore- and mainmasts, with lug topsails above, and a standing lug on the mizzen, sheeted to a long outrigger; a jib was set to a long running bowsprit. Such vessels were sailed by large, highly skilled crews and must have been a truly formidable sight when underway in a stiff breeze. By the 1770s a similar rig was also being used on northern French fishing boats but here the profile was shorter, the yards less peaked, no topsails were carried, and

These Cornish luggers seen in Mount's Bay are typical of the larger examples of the region with a dipping lugsail on the foremast and standing lug on the mizzen. Note that the mizzen mast on both boats nearest the camera, is set up to take a topsail; the steeply angled bumkin is typical of the Cornish lugger.

ABOVE Typical of the small working boats of northeast England, this Scarborough coble has a single large dipping lugsail (here reefed – perhaps for visibility) set on an aft-raking mast.

the mizzen could have a dipping, balance, or standing lugsail. A century later the northern French fishing rig would evolve to be more like the earlier naval version.

In Britain the Royal Navy used the lug rig on larger vessels with only a modicum of success – indeed, only one lugger was ever purpose-built, all others being captured – but did favour the rig in its small boats, gigs, and lifeboats. But the fishing communities adopted the rig as their own from about the 1780s, and used it in almost all coastal and offshore fisheries, as well as on small harbour boats and those serving shipping in the Channel and Irish Sea ports, Tyneside, and Thames Estuary. In the earliest boats the rig was three-masted, usually with square-headed dipping sails on the fore- and mainmasts, and with a standing lugsail on the mizzen. The rigs were short and powerful and grew in popularity for boats working on open waters and off beaches. By the early 1800s the two-master was becoming more popular. There are several possible reasons for this. First, the decline in smuggling meant a decline in the need for speed.

Secondly, the introduction of cotton as a sailcloth meant that sails could be lighter and therefore larger. Last, as fishing technology improved and catches increased, the mainmast became an inconvenience and was often lowered or even left ashore, its larger sail being taken forward and set on the foremast. By the middle 1800s the three-master had been displaced and the two-masted lugger had become the norm. Nevertheless, the origins of the type lingered on in the lugger's terminology: the two masts continued to be known as the 'fore', and 'mizzen'; there was no 'main' mast.

Although rig sizes and shapes varied around the British coast depending on size of hull and simple local preferences, the most common form of lugger was two-masted with a large dipping lugsail on the foremast and a smaller standing lugsail on the mizzen. The latter was typically sheeted to an outrigger, which in some areas had an exaggerated upward steeve. Masts were usually unstayed, with the sails' halyards doing the work of the windward shrouds.

Variations did occur from region to region. For exam-

THE LATEEN RIG

Similar to the dipping lugsail but with its head being the longest edge, the lateen sail originated in countries on the southern and eastern shores of the Mediterranean. It was appreciated in many regions and on many varied craft types, from fishing boats of southern Europe, to small boats of various international navies, and workboats of north America. It was adopted for the mizzen on square-rigged ships of the fifteenth century (see Full-Rigged Ship p.8) and as the principal sail of the three-masted Venetian galleys of the sixteenth and seventeenth centuries.

The traditional Arabic lateen had a flexible yard made up of two or three spars lashed together, whose overall length could be greater than that of the vessel itself. The forward end was bowsed down to the gunwale or stemhead leaving no space for a forestay; thus the mast was relatively short and heavy, and typically had a marked forward rake. Never an easy sail to handle, the long yard was liable to swing out of control, especially when tacking, and the rig required a large skilful crew.

Among the most famous, and notorious, of lateen-rigged craft were the three-masted xebecs of the Barbary coast pirates. They were often as long as 125ft, could be rowed as well as sailed, and were renowned for their manoeuvrability – their sailing abilities had considerable influence on the navies of France, Spain, and Britain who adopted many of their features. After about 1750 some xebecs incorporated square rig, but never to the exclusion of the lateen as principal sail.

In Spain, France, and Italy many coastal traders of the eighteenth, nineteenth, and early twentieth centuries carried a single-masted lateen rig with

In the late nineteenth century there were many lateen-rigged cargo carriers sailing on Lake Geneva. Their rigs, with twin, tall, slender sails, were perhaps among the most elegant of all sail plans.

staysail, jibs, and occasionally a jib-headed topsail. Such a rig was also much used on southern European fishing boats.

In England and northern Europe the lateen was less popular, perhaps partly because of the weight of the yard and the difficulties in reefing – the lateen sail is most usually reefed along its head to the yard. However, the lateen was used by at least three types of American working boats in the late 1800s. The seine netters of Apalachicola Bay and St George's Sound in Florida carried a single-masted lateen rig, and on the Piscataqua River (between New Hampshire and Maine) the gundalow had a single sail of lateen appearance, although it was really a jib-headed sail bent to a

yard-like mast stepped on a low post. But the most successful type was the felucca of San Francisco, a small double-ended boat with large lateen sail set on a forward-raked, unstayed mast, and with a jib set flying on a bowsprit that could be run inboard.

Today the lateen rig lives on in local craft of the southeast Mediterranean and is most impressively seen on the racing dhows of the United Arab Emirates.

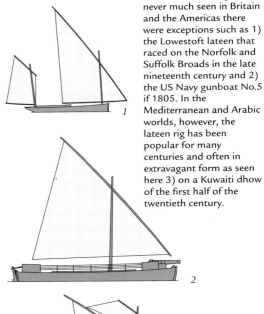

While the lateen rig was never much seen in Britain and the Americas there were exceptions such as 1) the Lowestoft lateen that raced on the Norfolk and Suffolk Broads in the late nineteenth century and 2) the US Navy gunboat No.5 if 1805. In the Mediterranean and Arabic worlds, however, the lateen rig has been popular for many centuries and often in extravagant form as seen here 3) on a Kuwaiti dhow of the first half of the twentieth century.

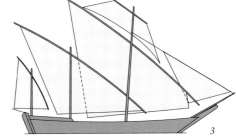

The Sennen Cove crabber is typical of the many small Cornish luggers of the nineteenth century. Her rig, though eminently simple, is large and powerful. The mizzen is an example of a standing lugsail – rarely used as the principal sail on a working boat.

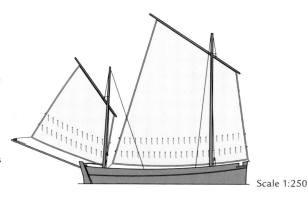

Scale 1:250

At first glance the sails of the French bisquine would appear to be dipping lugsails, however they were set standing, on alternating sides of the masts. These extraordinary vessels, with their three masts (the main and mizzen well raked) and multiple lug topsails, were unique to the Gulf of St Malo.

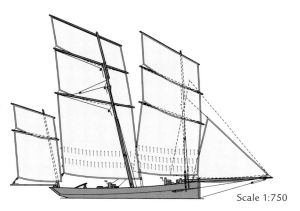

Scale 1:750

west as Falmouth in search of incoming ships – were two-masted with the common dipping fore and standing mizzen; they carried several different sails to suit all weather conditions and could set a jib to a short, reefing bowsprit and a topsail above the mizzen. The cobles of Yorkshire and Northumberland set a single large dipping lugsail on an aft-raking mast stepped well forward. The Scottish double-ended fifies and zulus set a large, tall, dipping-lug foresail and a standing-lug mizzen, with a light-weather jib sometimes set on a long-running bowsprit. On the West Coast of Scotland and northern England small 'whammel' boats used in river salmon fisheries set single standing lug-sails on short masts.

The coasts of Europe were similarly scattered with lug-rigged boats of varying size and design but probably none was more dramatic in appearance than the bisquines of the Gulf of St Malo. These extraordinary boats evolved from two-masted drift netters and dredgers. By the height of their development they were three-masted, the foremast stepped upright well forward in the eyes of the boat, the aft-raking mainmast amidships, and the mizzen mast just inboard of the stern, its sail sheeted to a long horizontal outrigger. All three masts carried standing lugsails with one or two lug topsails, and a massive jib was tacked to the long running bowsprit.

In working boats the lug rig never caught on in North America except in the waters of the Mississippi delta where the New Orleans lugger was much used in the late nine-teenth century. Unlike their European cousins these unique boats set a single dipping lugsail that was rarely dipped. Instead, a long horse was fitted in the bows and at the stern for the tack and the sheet, and when the yard was pressed against the mast the luff of the sail was hauled to wind-ward by means of powerful tackles in order to prevent it from backwinding, and the clew was sheeted in to flatten the sail as much as possible and to pull it off the yard; the mast was supported by a single shroud on each side.

Lugsails have been used in leisure craft for over 100 years – from the efficient fully-battened sails of the sailing canoes

ple, the early Scottish luggers carried two large dipping lugsails set well forward and aft; the large luggers of West Cornwall almost invariably set mizzen topsails; early Truro River oyster boats had a standing lugsail on the foremast with either a jib-headed or standing lugsail mizzen, nei-ther sail had a boom; harbour gigs of Falmouth, Fowey, and other busy Cornish ports set a dipping lug whose high-peaked yard extended way beyond the mast in lateen-like fashion; in East Cornwall, the mizzen was more likely to have a standing lugsail and a jib might be carried on a light-weight running bowsprit. In Hampshire, the Emsworth lugger set a single tall, narrow, square-headed dipping lug-sail and was rarely sailed to windward. The forepeakers of Deal in Kent – used as pilot boats and known to sail as far

THE CHINESE RIG

The true Chinese sail is a highly developed balance lug extended and stiffened by bamboo battens. It is set on a pole mast, hoisted by a single halyard; a parrel holds the yard to the mast and is used to help peak up the sail when reefed; each batten is similarly held to the mast and has a single-part rope leading to the mainsheet, each of these parts enables the sail to be flattened and is used when the sail is reefed – simply by lowering the sail as far as required into lazy jacks that are permanently set up on either side of the sail; two or more battens are lowered to lie along the boom and the now-lazy sheet parts are gathered up and tucked away. Such sails have been employed on Chinese vessels of all sizes for many centuries and, indeed, for many hundreds of years the technology was far in advance of anything seen in the West.

The Chinese rig was used on a diverse range of boat types – they varied widely in size and use from single-masted inshore craft, to large multi-masted seagoing traders. One of the most common arrangements was to step three masts: the mainsail was reduced in size, a foremast stepped right up forward carrying a large lugsail, and a mizzen stepped on a high poop deck. The mainsail's luff was kept vertical and did not greatly extend forward of the mast, while the

A Chinese lighter with two-masted 'junk' rig. Note the multiple-part sheet leading from each bamboo batten at the leech; not only does this arrangement improve the set under full sail but also, as can be seen here, simplifies sheeting when the sail is reefed.

foresail carried at least one third of its area forward of its mast. Depending on wind strength the vessel could sail with all three sails set, or just mizzen and foresail, or main and foresail. In the north, larger junks carried five masts, three of which were stepped on the centreline of the vessel and carried narrow tall sails with square heads and straight leeches; two mizzen masts were stepped on each quarter of the poop, the windward sail being set. To the south, sails were well peaked and the leech was rounded, only four or five battens were fitted.

As late as the 1960s there were many Chinese harbours with large sailing fishing fleets and some still work to this day. In China, Thailand, Hong Kong, and other parts of the region smaller sailing sampans are still commonly used for fishing, transport, and houseboats.

In the West 'junk-sail' derivatives can be seen on some modern cruising yachts and the type was made particularly famous in 1960 when Blondie Hasler competed in the first single-handed transatlantic race in *Jester,* an adapted Folkboat rigged with a single Chinese-type sail.

in the late nineteenth and early twentieth centuries, to the extreme racing sails of the lake yachts of Europe; from the simple but effective sliding-gunter rig of the ubiquitous Mirror dinghy to the standing lugsails of many a small knockabout boat of the late 1900s. (Curiously, while shunned by working boatmen, the lug rig has had a limited success in north America on sailing canoes and dinghies.) In working boats the rig went the way of all sail

in the face of motorised competition but with the 'traditional' revival of the late twentieth century, some fishing boats have been saved and restored to sail for leisure and educational use, while others, like the great bisquines *La Cancalaise* and *La Granvillaise*, and the more humble *An Sulaire* – a sgoth of the Isle of Lewis – have been newly built as replicas to preserve the dying maritime traditions of wooden boatbuilding and traditional seamanship.

CHAPTER 12

The Cat Rig

Ubiquitous on the coast of New England, the cat rig was briefly seen on nineteenth-century leisure craft in Britain and, unsuccessfully, on workboats of the San Francisco Bay area. Today it survives in varying forms on small American cruising boats and daysailers, as well as international racing dinghies.

DEFINITION

The cat rig is essentially the most simple of all sailing rigs: a single fore-and-aft sail set on an unstayed mast stepped as far forward as possible. Typically it is carried on a shallow-draughted hull of great beam, fine bow, and plumb ends: a catboat. But it may be set on less extreme hulls, although rarely on a deep-keeled heavy-displacement type. Traditionally, the sail was gaff-rigged, laced to a boom, and rigging was kept to a minimum: sometimes only one halyard and a sheet served for running rigging and there could be no standing rigging at all; at other times a forestay could be led to the stemhead, and a topping lift and gaff vang fitted to help control the sail when raising and lowering.

HISTORY

The cat rig may well have originated in the Netherlands where at least one type of shallow-draught working-boat type on the inland waterways set a single gaff sail hooped to a forward-stepped mast; but for more than 200 years it has been associated, almost exclusively, with the East Coast of America, specifically northwards from north New Jersey. In the early nineteenth century the rig was used on various keeled workboats, such as the short-gaffed point boats of Rhode Island, the Bahamas sharpshooter, open fishing boats of Nicaragua (where the rig was sliding gunter rather

than gaff), and the double-ended fish carriers of Eastport, Maine; but by the 1830s the archetypal shallow-draught catboat was emerging in the New York area.

As a working and fishing boat the type caught on fast: the simple rig was economical to set up; in relatively calm water it sailed well to windward – indeed, could only be out-performed upwind by a sloop with more generous sail area; it could be easily handled by one man; the beamy hull offered a stable working platform, ample space for load

---

The catboat varied in details but not in essentials – one large sail, usually gaff-rigged but occasionally jib-headed, stepped in the eyes of the boat.
1 A mid-nineteenth-century single-handed catboat from Newport, RI.
2 A catboat with small cuddy cabin built in 1881.
3 *Gracie* of the late 1800s, a catboat with bowsprit and jib (perhaps a cat-sloop).

4 A small cat-rigged dinghy with gunter-lug sail designed in 1923.
5 The famous children's dinghy/sail-trainer, the Beetle Cat, designed in 1921.
6 A typical working catboat of the North American east coast.
7 The Una Boat – the only cat-rigged boat to gain popularity in England (saving the Norfolk Wherry – see box) and even she was of American origin.

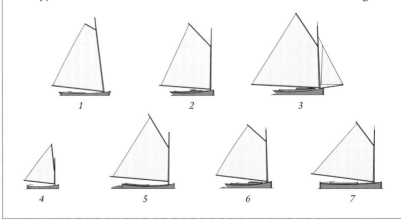

THE NORFOLK WHERRY

One of the most distinctive of British working craft, the Norfolk wherry could be described as cat rigged. Used to carry cargoes on the inland waterways of the Norfolk Broads the type was beamy and shoal-draughted – a 52ft boat would draw as little as 2ft 6in when unladen – and, like the American catboat, it set a single fore-and-aft boomless gaff sail on a stout mast stepped far forward. The mast had no shrouds but did have a single forestay. The Broads are crossed by bridges and it was vital for the wherry to be able to lower and raise its mast with ease. Thus the forestay was used as a hoisting line and the weight of the mast was counterbalanced by a piece of lead or iron – weighing as much as 300lbs – bolted to the foot. As they approached a bridge, the wherry's crew would brail the sail, lower the mast onto the deck hatches by releasing the forestay and pivoting the mast back in its tabernacle, shoot under the bridge, winch the mast back up with a pulley block at the bottom of the forestay, release the sail and sheet in – all in less than two minutes and without losing way. The sail had a single halyard and its sheet was led to an iron horse on the cabin top, forward of the helmsman.

The last trading wherry was built in 1912 but the type did not go out of service until the 1950s. Two have survived: the *Albion* (the only example to have been carvel rather than clinker planked) and the *Maud*. Several wherry yachts have also survived.

The Norfolk wherry's single forestay, with its block-and-tackle system at the foot allowing the mast to be easily raised and lowered while underway, is clearly visible in this photograph from the mid twentieth century. It is also interesting to note the three rows of reef points relatively low in the sail and close together – Norfolk wherries worked in relatively sheltered inland waters.

carrying, and with the mast stepped well forward the cockpit was left uncluttered for gear and catch. There were disadvantages, however. With no supporting shrouds relatively large-diameter heavy masts were stepped and, in even moderate seas, the exaggerated weight forward tended to bury the bow, especially when sailing downwind; if spilling wind the long overhanging boom could dip into a rising wave and drag the boat over to leeward; the narrow beam and small deck space at the mast step could lead to tricky sail-raising and -lowering in rough conditions; and unless quickly reefed the large single sail could give rise to considerable weather helm.

Thus, the catboat developed for use on shoal waters in sheltered areas. Typical were the bays on the south shore of Long Island, Narragansett Bay, Cape Cod, and Barnegat Bay. The earliest varieties had long shallow keels, little more than keelsons, and were known for being handy and reliable to windward. In the approaches to New York the boats quickly developed into wide, shallow, plumb-stemmed craft with a very shallow-v'd underbody and a large centreboard,

Conjurer, **designed and built by Crosby of Osterville, Massachusetts, in 1909, is a typical pleasure catboat of her day with large deep cockpit, small cabin cuddy forward, and barn-door rudder. She carries a single sail of 550sq ft on a 27ft hull with 12ft beam. Note the all-important topping lift for supporting the boom while raising and lowering the sail, and the provision for deep reefs. (Bejamin Mendlowitz)**

often as long as one-third of the hull length; on a 21ft boat a typical draught could be as little as 1ft 6in with the board raised, but increase to as much as 5ft when lowered. The working boats set moderate cat rigs in winter but in summer the mast could be stepped further aft, a long bowsprit shipped, and a jib set, transforming the rig from 'cat' to 'sloop' (see p.49). Under the large summer rig the boats became less stable and were known to capsize, but the helm was often better balanced.

More seaworthy types developed in Newport, Buzzards Bay, Martha's Vineyard, and around Nantucket, with probably the best known hailing from Cape Cod. Here, where the fisheries were more exposed, powerful boats of 18ft to 30ft in length were developed from about the 1870s for use in the lobster fishery and summer handlining; the sheer

was more pronounced and the bows higher to deal with the rougher conditions – a 28ft boat could have as much as 5ft freeboard at the stem. The rigs were kept moderate with efficient reefing gear led conveniently to the helmsman; such boats were known to be safe and able in most conditions. However, when the rig gained popularity in racing circles, sail areas were greatly increased with booms and gaffs becoming ever longer and less wieldy – in some boats the spars were so long that sails could only be reefed from a wharf or another boat. The height of the development undoubtedly led to a powerful rig but, when some of the racing refinements were adopted on cruising and even working cats the results were often tragic and the cat rig lost its once-high reputation.

The catboat type was tried away from New England waters but with mixed and only ever limited success. It was used in shrimping on the Gulf Coast of Florida for a while and introduced in the oyster fishery of San Francisco, but here the wind and sea conditions were too unforgiving and the rig was never popular. In the early 1850s a 16ft New York pleasure catboat called *Una* was shipped to London and sailed, almost unnoticed, on the Serpentine in Hyde Park. Then in 1853 she was moved to the Solent on the south coast where she was so admired that within a year a small fleet of 'Una boats' had been built. But, although highly regarded for its windward capabilities, in anything other than the calmest of seas the type gained a reputation for being at best wet, at worst dangerous.

Today the catboat remains locally popular in the waters of New England where it continues as a family sailing boat, favoured for its large roomy cockpit and initial stability. For American children the 12ft Beetle Cat, designed by Charles Beetle in 1921, has been one of the longest-lived training and club-racing boats, while further afield many modern plastic-moulded and fibreglass single-handed racing dinghies such as the Finn, Laser, Topper, or Sunfish have been developed with rigs that are essentially latterday developments of the cat rig – unstayed masts stepped well-forward setting single jib-headed sails.

Bibliography

Benham, Hervey *The Stowboaters* (Essex County Newspapers Ltd, Colchester, 1977)

Bennet, Douglas *Schooner Sunset, The Last British Sailing Coasters* (Chatham Publishing, London 2001)

Block, Leo *To Harness the Wind* (Naval Institute Press, Annapolis, MD, 2003)

Boell, Denis-Michel *Les Bisquines* (Le Chasse-Marée, Douarnenez, 1989)

Brewington, M V *Chesapeake Bay Bugeyes* (The Mariners' Museum, Newport News, VA, 1941)

Burgess, Robert H *Chesapeake Sailing Craft* (Tidewater Publishers, Cambridge, MD, 1975)

Cadoret, Bernard (ed) *Guide des Gréements* (Le Chasse-Marée, Douarnenez, 2000)

Carrick, Robert W & Henderson *Richard John G Alden and His Yacht Designs* (International Marine, Camden, ME, 1995)

Chapelle, Howard I *American Small Sailing Craft* (WW Norton, New York, NY, 1951)

——————*The History of American Sailing Ships* (WW Norton, New York, NY, 1935)

——————*The Search for Speed under Sail 1700–1855* (London, 1968)

Chapelle, Howard I. et al *The Catboat Book* (The Catboat Association with International Marine, Middleboro, MA, 1991)

Chapman, F H *Achitectura Navalis Mercatoria* (1768)

Clay, Jamie & Miller, Mark *Albert Strange on Yacht Design, Construction and Cruising* (The Albert Strange Association, Woodbridge, Suffolk, 1999)

Dunne, W M P *Thomas F. McManus and the American Fishing Schooners* (Mystic Seaport Museum, Mystic, CT, 1994)

Fontenoy, Paul E *The Sloops of the Hudson River* (Mystic Seaport Museum, Mystic, CT, 1994)

Gardiner, Robert *Warships of the Napoleonic Era* (Chatham Publishing, London, 1999)

Gilmer, Thomas C *A History of the Working Watercraft of the Western World* (International Marine, Camden, ME, 1994)

Greenhill, Basil (ed) *Sail's Last Century, The Merchant Sailing Ship 1830–1930* (Conway Maritime Press, London, 1993)

——————(ed) *Cogs, Caravels and Galleons* (Conway Maritime Press, London, 1994)

——————& Mannering, J (eds) *The Chatham Directory of Inshore Craft* (Chatham Publishing, London, 1997)

Kemp, Dixon *Manual of Yacht and Boat Sailing*, 8th edition (John Leather, ed) (Ashford Press Publishing, Southampton, 1988)

Kemp, Peter (ed) *The Oxford Companion to Ships and the Sea* (Oxford University Press, Oxford, 1992)

Kerchove, René de *International Maritime Dictionary*, 2nd edition (Van Nostrand Reinhold, New York, NY, 1961)

Lees, James *The Masting and Rigging of English Ships of War 1625–1860* (Conway Maritime Press, London, 1979)

Lavery, Brian *Jack Aubrey Commands* (Conway Maritime Press, London, 2003)

——————*The Ship of the Line,* Vols I & II (Conway Maritime Press, London, 1984)

László, Veres & Woodman, Richard *The Story of Sail* (Chatham Publishing, London, 1999)

Leather, John *Barges* (Adlard Coles, London, 1984)

——————*Gaff Rig* (Adlard Coles, London, 1970)

——————*Smacks and Bawleys* (Terence Dalton, Lavenham, Suffolk, 1991)

——————*Spritsails & Lugsails* (Adlard Coles, London, 1979)

MacGregor, David R *Clipper Ships* (Argus Books, Watford, 1979)

——————*Merchant Sailing Ships 1775–1815* (Argus Books, Watford, 1980)

——————*Merchant Sailing Ships 1815–1850* (Conway Maritime Press, London, 1984)

——————*Merchant Sailing Ships 1850–1875* (Conway Maritime Press, London, 1984)

——————*Square Rigged Sailing Ships* (Argus Books, Watford, 1977)

——————*The Schooner* (Chatham Publishing, London, 1997)

McGowan, Alan *HMS Victory, Her Construction, Career and Restoration* (Chatham Publishing, London, 1999)

March, Edgar J *Inshore Craft of Britain: In the Days of Sail and Oar* (Chatham Publishing, London, 2005)

——————*Sailing Drifters: Story of Herring Luggers of England, Scotland and the Isle of Man* (David and Charles, Newton Abbot, Devon, 1969)

Marquardt, Karl Heinz *The Global Schooner* (Conway Maritime Press, London, 2003)

McKee, Eric *Working Boats of Britain* (Conway Maritime Press, London, 1983)

Parry, M H et al *A Dictionary of the World's Watercraft, From Aak to Zumbra* (Chatham Publishing, London, 2000)

Rousmaniere, John *The Low Black Schooner* (Mystic Seaport Museum Stores, Mystic, CT, 1986)

Simper, Robert *The Forgotten Coast* (Creekside Publishing, Lavenham, Suffolk, 2002)

——————*The Lugger Coast*, (Creekside Publishing, Lavenham, Suffolk, 2003)

——————*The Sunrise Coast* (Creekside Publishing, Lavenham, Suffolk, 2002)

Smyth, H Warington *Mast and Sail in Europe and Asia* (John Murray, London, 1906)

Starkey, David J, Reid, Chris & Ashcroft, Neil (eds) *England's Sea Fisheries* (Chatham Publishing, London, 2000)

Stephens, Olin J *All This and Sailing, Too* (Mystic Seaport, Mystic, CT, 1999)

Underhill, Harold A *Deep-Water Sail* (Brown, Son & Ferguson, Glasgow, 1952)

——————*Sailing Ship Rigs and Rigging* (Brown, Son & Ferguson, Glasgow, 1938)

Winton, John *An Illustrated History of the Royal Navy* (Salamander Books, London, 2000)

Woodman, Richard *The History of the Ship* (Conway Maritime Press, London, 1997)

Index

Page numbers in bold indicate an illustration.